SURVIVING HELL 2

RETURN TO IRAQ

WORLDCON AWARDS
RECOMMENDED

DEMETER NORTH

Copyright @2023 by Demeter North

All rights reserved. No part of this book may be reproduced in any form or by any electronic or mechanical means, including information storage and retrieval systems, without permission in writing from the publisher, except by reviewers, who may quote brief passages in a review.

This publication contains the opinions and ideas of its author. It is intended to provide helpful and informative material on the subjects addressed in the publication. The author and publisher specifically disclaim all responsibility for any liability, loss or risk, personal or otherwise, which is incurred as a consequence, directly or indirectly, of the use and application of any of the contents of this book.

WORKBOOK PRESS LLC
187 E Warm Springs Rd,
Suite B285, Las Vegas, NV 89119, USA

Website:	https://workbookpress.com/
Hotline:	1-888-818-4856
Email:	admin@workbookpress.com

Ordering Information:
Quantity sales. Special discounts are available on quantity purchases by corporations, associations, and others. For details, contact the publisher at the address above.

Library of Congress Control Number:

ISBN-13:	978-1-960752-50-5 (Paperback Version)
	978-1-960752-52-9 (Digital Version)

REV. DATE: 03/13/2023

This book is a tribute to combat veterans who served with me in Camp Blue Diamond, Camp Baharia, Ramadi, and the outlying posts we were guarding and patrolling.

OUR HELL

The dark place in your mind is a disease, blight, a poison that never goes away. You try to be what passes for normal and you can for a while, but it always catches up with you. It starts with a tingle in your hands and a slight tremor; you feel it coming so you try to focus and steady your hands but it only makes it worse. You are unsure at this point what set it off, helpless to stop the rage from growing ever stronger, building, expanding, and encompassing your whole being. It is imperative to leave whatever you are doing to locate a safe place away from the people all around you. You feel as if you are suffocating, needles stabbing you all over your face the pain growing ever stronger. It is a struggle now to separate the nightmare from reality. You see flashes and glimpses of the horrors that feel so real you think you're in them all over again.

The battle is hard but you regain the necessary control it takes to pretend in front of the ones left around you. Your mind stops screwing around with you and you can begin to focus on the attempt at being normal again. You have to analyze what occurred, replaying the triggers and images trying to separate fact from fiction, searching for that exact point where it started so you can avoid it next time around. You pull out the pocket notebook you keep on you at all times and write down a few of the events that are still fresh trying to lobotomize them, the rest are still fuzzy. Once everything you could remember is on paper you put it away and continue with what you were previously doing. You look around but no one seemed to notice you had spaced out or stepped out for that matter. It is obvious to you that this hard won battle was fought with no one the wiser around you. In a way this makes you feel separated from them like they have no clue and could care less that there was a fight for your life going on right in front of them.

YOU HAVE FORGOTTEN

You Have Forgotten

I have wounds that you can not see

You have forgotten

My mind fights false sights, sounds and thoughts within me

You have forgotten

I'm betrayed everyday by minds broken being

You have forgotten

From the inside sometimes I'm cold callus and have no feeling

You have forgotten

I'm bottled up inside from anger, hurt, betrayal, and terror

You have forgotten

Once and again I'm crazy back again from a slip or minor error

You have forgotten

The nightmares inside are an exhausting daily struggle

You have forgotten

Fitting in with "normal" just to keep from trouble

You have forgotten

How I struggle with my soul and fight for you

You have forgotten

You think because I seem "ok" the battle is through

You have forgotten

Truth be told it's a new battle every day

You have forgotten

I'll never win the war of my mind until my life I pay

MY MIND

I'm tired of fighting my mind is almost done

The demons are knocking and I'm to far gone

A private war is waged inside my mind

This private war hurts every love I bind

A daily struggle I will one day let go

I don't want trouble just to be left alone

I'm desperate and craving but nothing satisfies

So much hate and fear I constantly traumatize

The meds kick in my mind now numb

I lost myself and am under delusions thumb

A temporary fix till I battle the next day

I quickly try to fix anything I might try to break

But there are to many causes of heart ache

So many things broken from the battle
before

I can't fix it all till the demons again at the
door

I pick someone so small to focus on and be
true

Of all the things I break I fight the hardest
its not you

I try to make sure your pain and suffering is
none

For once you are broken my battle is lost
and I am done

TABLE OF CONTENTS

INTRO

Laugh and the world laughs with you; cry and you cry alone.

Well, it is that time again, preparing for round two and on our way to Ramadi. I had Chap and Joker on board with me so this trip wouldn't be too bad I figured. This was a new unit we were attached to and there were a lot of good guys in it. I was thinking that I'm not such a bad influence (aside from my own drinking habits) and I don't get into much trouble anymore so this time will be better. Most of the guys just ignored me and I was fine with that. Chap still harassed me from time to time. He wanted me going out and playing sports, racket ball of all sports, I always dreaded playing him because no matter how much faster I was he still managed to beat me. (Personally I attribute it to his longer arms and legs of which I decided was a handicap for me since my speed could not hope to compete with his height.)

1

Thinking on the past few months I had pretty much drank away my spare time, the rest we trained and got ready for the deployment. I had gotten what they call Motto (that means being hard core marine like). I'm not sure if it was the blood stripe or knowing I was going back to Iraq again that gave me motto. Chap hadn't seemed to have changed much; He appeared to be more of a jerk to the folks around him but he never acted that way towards me that I noticed. I guess battle buddies are immune to that sort of thing with each other. As for Joker, he was pretty laid back, his quick witted comments and jokes (hence the nick name) kept a good mood in the air for us. Once again I discover Chap had known Joker for a while, it always seemed that everyone I met was already friends with Chap. We all bonded over a few nights out and just clicked like we belonged together.

A few of the other guys had started to grow on me as well. There was Tank. He was a pretty hefty guy and man could he down a beer. But he was good company and had a level head even for a boot. Then there was Frank. He was like a lost puppy dog that just seemed to follow you everywhere. All he ever wanted to do was play poker with us whenever we had a game going and just wanted to be part of "our group". I tried to keep my distance but it was hard and people tend to grow on you after a while. That and I've found specific circumstances build bonds even if you don't want them. We would be headed into what I began calling "Hell" together. (I didn't call it hell back then but it's like a hell now for some of us that went.)

I thought I was ok. I drank and kept to myself. I didn't cause any trouble. The nightmares seemed to go away but there were rare occasions I had anger issues for what seemed to be no reason. I found shutting off my emotions (which I was really good at now) was the easiest way to cope and deal with anything, that and I drank a lot to forget most things deliberately.

We were ready; this was going to be a good trip for us. It was hard acting normal or being sane around other people who just didn't get it couldn't understand. It was almost as if going back was a relief, no more pretending to be what I found I couldn't be anymore. The people who knew and understood would be around me with no judgments and I could have a moment and no one batted an eye. That it was the normal for us.

1

CHARACTER IS A HABIT LONG CONTINUED

We landed in Kuwait to prep for the final leg to Iraq. Nothing had changed since the last time we were there. I had almost forgotten how damn hot it was. The air hadn't changed one bit. Even at a different time of year it was still a smoking 130*F. Chap had been harassing a few of the boots making them sweep the sand in the hut we were staying in. I tried not to laugh too hard at their futile efforts.

I hadn't seen Joker since we had landed not sure where he went off to. Chap was preoccupied although watching was entertaining enough for me. My attention for that sort of sport was short. It was a part of the culture that bonded everyone but that didn't mean I had to participate in it.

As soon as I got the chance I headed to the farthest part of the base I could get to and climbed up the wall. I'm not sure what I wanted to achieve up there aside from being alone. I felt calm when I made it to the top I looked out and all I saw was barren empty land, almost nothing all the way to the horizon. I had gotten up there just in time to watch the sun set.

Looking across the distance it almost reminded me of a part of Texas a buddy and I drove through visiting his family. I sat for a moment savoring the peace and enjoying the lonely landscape. When the Sun was gone I hopped down from my perch and turned to go, I saw Frank standing there with his hands in his pockets just watching me looking a little lost.

I chucked inside but I didn't show that I was amused as I spoke, "How long have you been there?" Frank responded, "As long as you Corporal." I responded, "You following me now?" Frank was quick to respond, "No!

Well not intentionally... You've been here before. I just wanted to see what you did around here." I let him see me crack a smile as I gestured for him to follow me. Frank quickly fell in line behind me to go where ever I decided to head.

It didn't take Frank long to start talking as we walked. He talked about his family in Oklahoma and his Fiancée. How they were going to get married when he got back. He talked about his younger brother and how he was going into high school. I could see in his eyes as he spoke he was attempting to pour out his story and get some kind of approval of who he was and be accepted. As he kept talking I just nodded my head at the points that needed a response and finally reached my destination. I sat on a table on the complete opposite side of the base we were just on. I figured Frank would have lost interest as we walked but I could see he wasn't giving up. At this point most of his speech was muttering, sort of like the teacher talking in those Charlie Brown cartoons (wawa wha wa wha wa wha) I was no longer paying attention lost in my own thoughts of how this place made me feel.

Then out of no where Frank caught my attention with a question, "Corporal... why aren't you hanging out with other NCO's like the other NCO's do?" I responded sharply with, "I hang out with Chap." Frank thought for a second before speaking again, "No, I've watched you. You are with Chap, but you never hang out like friends. You just sit and watch TV, play pool or poker and don't talk. Plus he is the only one I've ever seen you even spend time with."

I paused for a moment before speaking in an irritated tone, "What is it you are looking for or want?" Frank seemed confused by the question but answered anyway, "Nothing I was just trying to figure you out. I didn't mean anything by it." I gave him a glaring stare as if to burn a hole in his face but he didn't flinch or blink. After a few seconds I started talking as I walked away, "You don't have to have a conversation to enjoy some ones company that you respect, just being in the same area is enough sometimes." I paused long enough to give him the hint of silence being golden.

Time passed and not sure how much time it was that had gone by while I sat at the table quietly with Frank but the silence wasn't going to last any longer. Frank spoke in a quiet voice as if to avoid angering me, "Corporal?" I replied, "What Frank?" He quickly responded, "You're almost out of smokes and I was wondering if you were hungry... We could stop by the USO and then the chow hall if that's ok." I replied with a sigh, "Sure Frank."

It was apparent at this point Frank wasn't going anywhere without me and being his Squad Leader I felt I was responsible for his morale and wellbeing. We left for the USO and then to the Chow Hall. Nothing had changed in this place. The only thing I noticed were how few people there were on base this time compared to what seemed forever but was only a few months ago when I was here last time going home.

It was getting late and it had been quite some time since I had any alcohol in my system. I had started to notice a slight tremor in my left hand. It only shook when I grabbed something or switched hands to smoke, but it was enough to get me to start clenching my left hand every now and then to keep it under control. I had lost track of time and didn't even notice that Frank had left me already.

I headed back to where the tents were. I saw Chap sitting on a fold out chair outside the entrance smoking. I sat in the sand next to him and he handed me a cigarette and lighter. As I started lighting my smoke Chap started talking, "Where'd you go all day?" I responded, "Around." Chap smirked at the vague comment but lightly kicked sand at me to show he wanted more detail.

I inhaled deeply and partially held my breath to get a light nicotine rush before speaking,

"I climbed up the outer wall to get a good view outside the Kuwait base and just think. I got interrupted by Frank who seemed to tag along the rest of my day." Chap laughed as he spoke, "Cute." I attempted to push his chair over but decided after a few seconds of pushing that chap was heavier than I remembered and I wasn't willing to put more effort into knocking him in the sand.

We sat smoking a few cigarettes before going to sleep. You could tell everyone was amped up about going to Iraq. It was most every one's first tour. I was indifferent at this point. I knew I would enjoy the money being tax free and the extra $200 for combat pay. I wasn't looking forward to playing politics anymore. We were too involved last time.

As I looked at Chap I could tell he had been through as much as I had. His look was stern and straight. His attention was on all the sounds and movement around him. His senses were heightened just being here again. His hands if you watched closely had a faint shimmer to them but only visible if you knew to look for it. He hid his symptoms almost as well as I did.

I figured this place would be the death of us this time. As we sat quietly I came to the realization that I was so tired of fighting myself and trying to be normal. I wouldn't be too upset if I died here, a warrior's death in my mind was as glorious as it got. I played a few scenarios out in my mind as I sat there lost in my downward spiral, I imagined myself taking hits and going as far as I could taking as many out as I could before dropping. Once again time passed without me realizing it as my daydream took over my life. I suddenly caught a punch to the shoulder. Chap was looking at me as I recovered and stood up. I yelled out, "Fuck you!" I could see Chaps scowl as he started speaking, "I know that look you just had. Whatever you are thinking don't, I don't care what it was about but I know you and... just fucking don't."

I sat back down and let the punch slide, I

guess I deserved it. I had been around Chap too long for him not to notice when I was thinking in the wrong direction. Not sure what gives it away every time but somehow he always seemed to know.

The days seemed to be a lot hotter and longer in Kuwait than I remembered. The last time we were only here a short while, this time we were here a few days before moving on. There had been a few incidents apparently near the base we were going to that delayed our trip.

I started to wonder if it was better or worse than it was before. It was kind of hard to imagine it getting worse. A few reports we had been reading showed the insurgents had been getting better at placing IED's and that they were more dangerous. We also heard reports of them being smuggled in by the dozens. It seemed as if there was a never ending line of cockroaches invading, whenever you killed one apparently more showed up in the house. I was beginning to wonder if the local population was ever going to defend themselves from the abuse they had been taking with the insurgents. It did help to know that at least we gave them a fighting chance against their abusers. We were going to be working with the Iraqi police and government this time. So that was a good sign and a step in the right direction to make a difference for these people.

As my thoughts trailed off Chap gave me a nudge and went inside the Hut and I followed. Everyone was lying in their racks either listening to their head phones, playing cards or sleeping. I decided at this point I was going to be one of the sleepers and lay in the rack where one of the boots in my squad had placed my gear.

I must have been tired because when I woke up it was bright out and I don't remember dreaming anything. It had been a long time since I had gone without a nightmare so it was nice not to remember anything. I figured it was going to be a good day and set out in a better mood than I had been in a long while.

As I was walking I noticed Frank wasn't too far behind me. I could tell he was trying to keep his distance trying to decide how he was going to approach me and not get yelled at. So I yelled out before he made a move, "Come here Frank! I'm not blind!" Frank responded, "Yes Corporal! Sorry Corporal!" I Responded, "Don't Sorry me get the fuck up here!"

Frank sprinted to my side and started walking in stride with me. I spoke as soon as he was in step, "What's going on Frank?" He carefully thought of his words before speaking, "I thought I would follow you and help you with anything you needed Corporal." I frowned and spoke, "kissing my ass isn't going to get you any special treatment boot." Frank panicked slightly and responded quickly, "no Corporal, that's not my intention I swear!"

I looked him in the eyes and decided his comment was genuine so I let him follow me. I began to speak to set him at ease, "You can follow me but on one condition." Frank excitedly responded, "Anything Corporal!" I spoke again, "You follow, you listen, you watch, you learn, and you're for the most part silent." Frank tried to hold back his smile as he responded, "Of course Corporal I promise!"

I headed to the market place to waste some time. Kuwait had a lot of nice shops if I remember correctly just needed to wander around and find the market. We flew out in the morning and I didn't want to be idle and have time to think. Keeping busy kept my mind quiet.

The first shop was a tent that had all kinds of hand made rugs. I was a little shocked at the several hundred to thousands of dollars that they had as a price on them. I wondered who in their right mind would want one let alone spend that kind of money on one.

The next shop was in a wooden shack, it looked hastily put together. How ever I did find objects of interest in this tent. I had never seen a hookah before and wasn't sure how to use it but decided if it was still here when I returned I would get one.

The next few were clothing stores which I decided to skip. I also skipped the jewelry stores and the house ware stores. Frank at this point hadn't said a word but I could tell he spotted something he liked and whatever it was had his attention in front of us.

I spoke to open the conversation, "What's on your radar Frank?" Frank responded, "There's local food carts ahead, is the food here good?" I answered, "To be honest I'm not sure. But if you want to stop and try some I'm game."

We walked up to the carts and Joker and Chap were already at one trying some of the local meats. Frank walked ahead of me and started talking to the guy at the goat cart selling the food on his grille. I walked over to Joker and Chap and spoke, "You guys are going to get the runs from that shit." Chap responded, "Whatever. With all the MRE's were about to eat again on patrols it will even out the constipation."

Joker laughed and patted me on the back. Relax buddy. Enjoy what's here while you can. I laughed and cracked a smile thinking he was right. I was being too uptight. By this time Frank was back at my side handing me sticks of meat.

Chap laughed and said, "Eat and join us in a dire(pause)rea situation." Frank had a confused look on his face. I responded at frank to educate him on the conversation, "It tastes good but you're going to shit a lot... comprehindae?" Frank just smiled and took a big bite of the meat on the stick.

Chap looked at frank and started talking, "So what's with the following the leader routine boot?" I spoke before Frank could, "First of all he's my boot so leave him alone. Screw with yours all you want. Secondly his company is welcome and I am allowing him to tag along." Chap waived his hands in the air in a back off gesture as he spoke, "Hey, ok don't get your panties in a wad I was just asking."

Frank seemed to beam at my comment but didn't say anything due to being surrounded by NCO's. Frank, now trailing behind, still kept in step following Joker, Chap and I as we walked through the rest of the market.

I started to think about how I snapped to Franks defense and why as we were walking. Normally I would have let Chap pick on whomever. I wasn't sure yet why, maybe I could sense he didn't fit in or maybe he reminded me of myself at an earlier point in my life, I wasn't sure.

The rest of the day seemed to drift by fairly fast. Joker had to go check on his squad and make sure they were packed and so did Chap so they were no longer with me. I however hadn't felt like baby sitting so I wrote a note stating Frank was on orders to get everyone ready in my squad and let him do it. He seemed eager to please and hopefully it would make the others pay attention to him. Either that or make them dislike him more.

I wasn't sure of the outcome but I would find out soon as I was headed back to the hut. When I got inside I was slightly impressed and to be honest relieved. My guy's bags were packed and ready to go. The room was clean and tidier than when we came in. Sand was still everywhere but there was nothing we could do about that.

I looked at Frank as he sat and the rack gave him a pat on the back and said good job loud enough for the others to hear me give him praise. Frank smiled and nodded then went back to writing in what looked like a journal.

I headed to my bunk and lay down to go to sleep. It was going to be an early morning for the last plane ride to Iraq. I wanted to make sure I was well rested for the journey to base. My thoughts seemed to drift into past memories of the last time as it was now a full realization that we were going back.

As I slowly drifted to sleep I could feel my body and hear sounds but couldn't move. It felt as if I weighed ten times my normal weight. I knew my brain was acting up so I ignored my senses and forced my mind to be empty. It was all in my head and I shut it off and finally drifted to sleep.

2

DEATH NEVER TAKES A WISE MAN BY SURPRISE HE IS ALWAYS READY TO GO

As I awoke to fire watch coming around getting everyone up to leave I had a strong urge to smoke but when I checked my wrist watch we didn't have much time to spare so I decided it would have to wait.

I had done this song and dance before and was not looking forward to the C-130 ride. I hate it when I get airsick so I downed the highest amount of motion sickness pills the bottle directed and told myself I should be fine this time around. The last thing I wanted was to be embarrassed in front of boots.

I got my squad together and in line. They had already made the racks and their bags were on their shoulders ready to go. As we came out of the hut we fell in line with the rest of the battery and all started the walk back to the tarmac for the flight out.

Everyone started loading our bags and equipment we brought into the quad con designated for us and we packed ourselves into the C130 for the flight out. All we had on us were our helmets, flack jackets, rifles, and other miscellaneous gear we put in our backpacks for the ride. I remembered what happened last time we landed but I was almost positive that wouldn't happen twice.

The flight was just as rough this time as it had been the last. I started to think the pilots were screwing around with us trying to get people sick. Amazingly enough no one got sick and we landed without any issues.

Our convoy was on the tarmac waiting to pick us up. We went straight from the plane to the convoy and loaded our weapons with the ammunition they had ready for us. It was almost an adrenalin rush just being loaded up with ammo again.

The Marines on the convoy looked like they had been here for a while. A few had small holes wearing into their uniforms and the color was fading from the sun. They seemed stiff and emotionless but that was something I had gotten used to from the last time I was here.

It didn't take long for us to be loaded and on our way. As the convoy drove out of the base I couldn't help but have second thoughts about coming here again. I couldn't abandon my friends so I quickly brushed the thought away. I was here for them nothing more. Do my job and go home. That's the plan at least.

The trip to Ramadi was silent almost eerie like. I was expecting something to happen the whole way. Despite my gut feeling that something was off nothing happened for the entire trip to the base. I guess you get lucky every now and then and nothing happens at all.

When we got on base the transition was more streamlined than last time. The convoy dropped us off and was already loading up the marines leaving the base. We headed to the same buildings Chap and I had stayed at last time. Only this time we weren't able to stay together. We roomed with our current squads.

The building I was in was closer to the towers of the base this time. However this was the building I stashed all the alcohol on the roof the first tour. I was curious to see if the stuff I left was still there. I would have to find out when things settled down.

As I sat in the hutch I noticed everyone in my squad was watching what I was doing and where I placed everything. I snapped my fingers and motioned for them to move in. When the last of them circled around I started to speak. In line from left to right in my squad were Frank, Hart, Daniels, Jarred and Vince.

"Pay attention, this is vital and important

so you can have more down time and less preparation time. See how my gear is organized on the floor and my gear box. I want yours to look the same, all the gear is organized from left to right in the order which you put in on and when you take the gear off you place it in reverse order right to left, so that it remains the same. Got it?" The unified response was, "Yes Corporal."

I don't know why but I always seemed to have to fight a slightly devilish smile when my guys responded to me like that.

Not too long after that another Marine came in to hand me our job duties and orders. It came in a manila envelope. I wasn't surprised when I opened it to find we were on tower duty. However I was curious why it stated we were escorting base sweepers.

As I read it aloud one of the guys in my squad, Hunter, asked at the end, "What's a base sweeper?" I responded cryptically, "I'm not sure to be honest but I guess we will find out what it is at 10:00 AM tomorrow morning.' I then ended with, "Rest day is Saturday so make sure you plan to relax wisely now go do something productive and stay out of trouble."

The squad acknowledged my order and took off in several directions I assume to explore the base but I wasn't sure nor did I care at the moment. As I sat down I could hear that lovingly boom sound of a reminder that I was back in Iraq. It was the pounding of a mortar I could hear through the window as it came down and impacted on the roof of the building next to me. Not even a second later another round hit somewhere not too far from the first.

I laughed to myself as I could hear swearing and what was probably my squad hitting the dirt. I sighed and thought that never gets old and always makes me laugh. I tried to think of why but the only answer I could get was the image of the feeble attempt of diving and avoiding being hit, the sand in the face as you go down, maybe that was what made me chuckle every time.

I brushed off my thoughts and prepped my schedule. We had towers one and two at the front of the base as well as the .50 Cal shack outside the gate. I had to figure out which one of my guys had enough balls to man the .50cal in the shack all by himself at night.

The problem with the shack is only one person could man it and you were outside of the base and the defense of a suicide bomber from the front gate was you. You were also the best target for mortar fire and snipers due to being out in the open. I decided to man it myself for now and will see who does it after a few weeks.

After drafting up a schedule I placed a copy on everyone's rack and headed out. As I started to walk around I noticed someone was hanging around a shutdown tower by the south gate and went over to see who it was, I noticed it was Chap.

As I came over Chap started to speak, "They

didn't even fix the fucking tower." I looked at the rubble at the top. I thought about responding but couldn't find the words so I lit a cigarette and handed it to Chap and lit another for myself.

We stood there smoking for what felt like an hour and only started walking because we had to go to the USO to get more smokes. As we walked I started talking, "My boys and I got front towers how about you?" Chap chucked as he spoke, "I got convoy and patrols again." I responded, "Shitty." Chap responded back, "Yeah…"

We got to the USO and it had been silent for a while. Joker came up and dumped sand down both our shirts as he came up behind us and started talking, "You ass holes not only didn't wait for me but didn't try to come find me either." Chap kicked sand at Joker and I tried to get the sand to go through my pants and out the leg in an awkward shake like dance.

Joker just laughed and walked with us. I

spoke as we walked, "Ass clown, that shits going to be on me all day now…" Joker responded, "Maybe you won't forget next time." Chap chuckled and spoke, "Yeah it was a good one."

As we started walking to the chow hall an alarm went off I hadn't heard before. Not even 10 seconds into the alarm a few HMMWV's sped through the road past us toward the front gate. Chap looked at me and spoke, "That was new." I responded," Wonder what that is for."

Joker spoke up as we got close to the Chow hall, "So how does this whole schedule thing work as far as hanging out goes." Chap responded, "We hang out when we can but otherwise we pretty much don't see each other for a while at a time." Joker responded, "That sucks."

Chap looked at me as we walked through the chow hall doors and spoke, "You have the same plan as last time?" I responded, "Better plan this time." Jim bean shipped regularly in drop bottles. They hold a full shot and should make it through the mail system." Chap smiled as he spoke, "Nice! Only for us this time ok?" I laughed as I spoke, "I hear you I don't plan on sticking us into trouble this time."

Joker looked interested in the back story as he spoke, "This time?" Chap responded, "Long bad story of this guy (Chap points at me) sticking his hands into to many cookie jars and pissing off the wrong people."

Joker started to laugh as we stood in line to get our food. The chow hall had changed a little since we had been here. Now there were flag decorations everywhere but nothing else seemed to change.

It still had the same buffet lines for food and the sign still said they had steak and seafood nights too. I filled my plate with salad as I used to do, lettuce, cucumbers, diced ham, tomatoes topped off with shredded cheese ranch dressing and bacon bits.

As Chap sat down he had nothing but a plate full of sliced meats and cheese. Joker sat and his plate was full of an assortment of fruit and sandwiches. It amazed me how different our preferred tastes were. I can't recall a time other than drinking that all three of us actually wanted the same thing.

All three of us went back for more a few times before deciding our stomachs were full. Joker spoke as he stood, "Well boys I guess we'll see each other when we do. I have duty at the Mechanics shop so you can find me there whenever you want." Chap and I nodded. Then Joker left.

Chap grabbed my shoulder as we started to walk out, "Don't be stupid this time I won't be there to help you out. Promise me?" I lightly smiled as I spoke, "No more stupid than usual." I then brushed his hand off and gave him a false salute as I went in the opposite direction he was going.

I started to mumble under my breath as I walked, "Don't be stupid, blah-blah-blah, fuckoff." As I was about to continue my one way conversation Frank chimed in, "Don't be stupid about what Corporal?" I spoke, "Shit Frank, You going to let me know when you're eavesdropping next time or what?"

Frank spoke, "Sorry Corporal, I didn't mean too. No one else wanted to hang out with me so I came and found you." I responded, "What do you mean no one wanted to hang out with you?" Frank answered in a depressed voice, "Everyone thinks I'm weird and annoying."

I couldn't help but feel for Frank so I spoke, "Look bud you're not weird and annoying. Did I chase you off?" Frank responded, "No corporal." I spoke again, "You're in MY squad and you are one of MY boots, no one else's, you got that? Someone gives you a hard time I want to know about it. Okay?" Frank at this point had a slight smile on his face as he spoke, "Yes Corporal, Thank you Corporal!"

Frank followed behind me as I continued to walk to the bunk house we were staying in. When we got to the bunk house Hart,

Daniels, Jarred and Vince were already back getting ready to sleep because tomorrow's shifts were going to be early.

I came in and told frank to stand in the doorway. I began to yell, "Get on your feet you ass wipes!"(Everyone began scrambling off the racks to put their boots on and stand up) So you want to alienate our light machine gunner do you? (I flipped the first set of racks onto the floor) Who do you think is going to save your ass with cover fire on patrols out here? (I flipped over the second set of racks and still no one made a sound) Who do you think could potentially save your life when you're wounded and call for help? (I decided not to flip the last set of racks due to Franks stuff being on it) I want you guys to take a good look at Frank. See the m249 SAW that he's hauling around? That's life saving fire power and in a fight the man with that weapon is your best friend."

I gave them a moment to think on my words before I continued, "Who wants to go home alive? (Still no one spoke) If you want to go home alive I suggest making friends with Frank cause without him you probably won't make it. Now clean up this mess. Help them out frank." Frank responded, "Yes corporal."

Everyone cleaned up the disaster I made of the bunk house. I could however tell the tone of the room changed. Frank was now playing poker with Daniels and Jarred. I was satisfied that I got my point across. The statements might not be entirely true unless we went on patrols but I wasn't looking to switch our duties at the moment.

Once the poker game was done everyone went to sleep. The mosque music was now more audible with everything quiet. I however was prepared this trip and put plugs in my ears. I slowly drifted to sleep as my mind started drifting off.

3

THE GREATEST REMEDY FOR ANGER IS DELAY

Tower duty was going well. Daniels proved gutsy enough to man the .50 Cal post on his own so I let him do it for now. I figured I would rotate everyone out on it eventually to make it fair. My first night out on the post and I had to Stab a damn rabid dog. They are everywhere and try to pack attack anything alone. Not sure if I killed it but I don't think it would come back.

I think everyone thought I made the story up to scare them for the post. They didn't seem to take me seriously when I told them to watch out for the packs of dogs. They would find out on their own or they might not. It mattered little to me.

I kept playing it out in my mind because I had to write a report on it later if it turned out that someone owned the dog. We would have to pay for the damages. I was just outside the post watching through the night vision goggles when the three dogs came out of the bushes.

I think they legit thought they could kill and eat me. I radioed in if I could shoot my shot gun but got a negative from control. So when the first dog jumped at me I hit him like a baseball with the shot gun swinging.

The second dog at that point came at me but I got a good kick into his face and by that point I had my knife out and had stabbed either the first dog or the third one I wasn't to sure but he Yelped loud enough that it got a spot light on us from tower one and two other marines came out to see what had happened.

They just laughed at me when they got to me. I flipped them the bird and went into the .50 Cal post to wait out the rest of the shift. The rest of that night was uneventful and we had gotten off at 2:00 AM. I only got 7 hours of sleep before sweep watch duty but that was more than enough.

I was heading to my morning detail of sweep watching. It was the damnedest thing I have ever been assigned to. I didn't even know what it was until we showed up the first day. You have 3 armed marines to baby sit six local Iraqi civilians who are literally sweeping the streets of the base with push brooms. Hence, sweep-watch duty.

Not only that. It HAS to take them 8 hours to do it no more and no less. So you have to watch the clock and make sure they stay on pace. I did notice that when I went back to the south gate where we had started it was as if nothing had been done.

I thought what a waste of American tax dollars, for crying out loud, we pay them to sweep a street that doesn't need sweeping in the first place. They did however try to get buddy-buddy with me pretty quick. I found out very fast if I wanted some contraband like alcohol these were the guys to get it.

I was getting curious though. One of them on the sweep detail wouldn't show however we were supposed to mark him down as if he did. So he got paid but never came. I began to wonder what scandal we were actually running here. I think the sweep detail was a cover. But I promised Chap to keep my nose clean so I would for now. At least until I talked to him about it.

I cleared my mind of those thoughts as I approached the sweep detail and signed them all in. Frank and Vince passed out the brooms and we started the timer. As they were sweeping Omar grabbed my arm and opened my hand.

I gave him an evil look however he continued what he was doing and ignored my look as he began to speak, "Look, look, you like? Girlfriend or wife like? I get more?" He eagerly waited for a response as I looked in my hands. He had placed several, what looked to be, fairly expensive pieces of jewelry into my hands.

I put them back into his pocket and spoke, "They look nice Omar but I am getting divorced." Omar spoke, "Daughter? Cousin? Mother maybe?" I could hear the desperation to sell them in his voice and I spoke again, "How much?" Omar answered, "For you Four Hundred." I looked at the jewels again then spoke, "Three hundred" Omar smiled and shook my hand as he spoke again, "Deal! You no regret I swear. I have lot more what you like?" I laughed and responded, "No more for now Omar get back to sweeping."

Frank came over to see what I bought and spoke, "I thought we were told to keep our distance? It says so in our order sheet." I smiled a little as I responded, "How much information do you think those guys have on the locals and what goes on off base Frank?"

Frank looked confused so I continued, "I bet they know quite a bit of information that we probably need. Why else would they be here sweeping the streets for money?" Frank spoke up, "I thought it was for charity for the locals." I responded, "If it was for charity it would be different people every time. These guys have name brand cloths that no one here can afford. They are into something different and I think I want in."

It felt like forever before we were at the front gate and the eight hours were up for the sweeping detail. As they handed the brooms back to Frank and Vince Omar stopped and spoke, "I bring you gift next week you like you buy." He then turned and left.

I needed to find where Chap was so I could ask a few questions on where his patrols went and what he thought about what I was thinking of doing. I think I had a plan and good Idea but here I would need to make sure more people were with me on it.

Chap must have been pretty busy because no matter when or where I looked he had already been there and gone. No one had an answer for when he was back or where he would be. So I gave up on waiting for him and decided I was going to be bold and act on my own.

I decided my initial goal was to find out where Shamir was when he was supposed to be on detail. My secondary goal was, what exactly could I get away with on getting information or things from these guys? All they seemed to want to do was get me something for the American money I had so all I had to do was find out what was worth me giving them money for what I wanted. That seemed simple enough. I would wait until Omar gave me my gift and I would purchase it regardless of what it was to put him in a good mood and that should be sufficient enough to at least buy information from him.

Until then I needed to find out who all dealt with the sweeping detail so I could keep an eye out for trouble in that direction. I didn't want to ruffle any feathers like I did last time. I learned my lesson and planned to be a lot more cautious now.

I wonder what Joker is doing? I'll go find him since I can't find Chap. He's probably been board to death without our company anyways. I started to head towards the south gate where the repair yard was, I assumed he should be there. Once again I noticed Frank was tagging along and with a mental shrug I gestured for him to get closer and he did.

When we got to the mech yard a few guys were working on different vehicles but I didn't see Joker. When I asked around I was told he was out driving in a convoy. Frank looked at me and spoke, "No luck today Corporal. Looks like you're not finding anybody."

I frowned dispiritedly and started heading to the chow hall. I was hungry and food always was a comfort for me. It looked as if I was going to be on my own this time around, everyone was busy with their own duties and our schedules just didn't seem to line up.

As we were walking to the chow hall mortar rounds started landing on the base. After the second mortar exploded the siren started going off. I turned around and looked at Frank huddled inside one of the side bunkers for cover.

Frank looked at me and I think I could literally see his teeth chattering as he spoke in a loud hurried voice, "There's room Corporal get in!" I couldn't help it, I had to chuckle before I spoke, "I'm getting food you coming or not." Frank hesitated before he spoke, "But mortars are falling." I responded, "They already fell, and they never fire more than two or three rounds. Our artillery hits them after three and they know that. Let's go eat."

Frank slowly got out and looked into the sky for a moment then hurried to my side again. As I started to walk Frank fell in step with me and we continued to the chow hall. I could tell that he was nervous but he trusted my judgment and did not question me about whether or not it was ok.

As we sat to eat in the chow hall I had my usual salad and frank had sandwiches and some bean thing I had never seen before. I spoke as Frank took a bite of what to me looked unappetizing, "What is that, like a bad day burrito? It looks like it came out of my ass."

Frank almost spit his food out as he tried not to laugh too hard and responded, "It's a Burrito Suizo! I hadn't eaten one since Puerto Rico! Isn't this great, I love this chow hall it's way better than on base in the states!" I started laughing at Franks excitement and spoke, "I agree little buddy it is way better. It is too bad we couldn't just bring the chow hall home with us that would be awesome."

I decided at that point to get to know frank better and spoke, "So where are you from Frank?" Frank answered, "Originally Puerto Rico but my family moved to New York and joining the marines was the fastest way to become an American citizen."

Frank started smiling and I could tell he was proud of his story I took that into consideration as I responded, "Your parents must be very proud of you." Frank responded, "Yes they are. (Frank smile got wider as he talked) I'm the first in my family to be in the military."

I lightly smiled then spoke, "That is something to be proud of Frank." Frank spoke again, "My family is proud, not just because I serve, but because I help support them and we are saving money to bring my fiancé and grandparents to America as well."

I smiled again to show I was happy for him and spoke, "I hope they all get to the states soon then buddy. You and your family deserve it." Frank just smiled and continued eating the burrito and then polished off the sandwiches on his plate.

We were done so we started heading back to the bunk house and as we got closer, I handed a piece of folded paper I had written a note on earlier to Frank and spoke, "Put this in Chaps bunk for me will ya?" Frank didn't even respond or blink he just took it and ran towards Chaps bunk house.

I was starting to get worried about Chap and Joker. I didn't like not knowing where they were or what they were doing. It's not that I'm a control freak or worried or anything, okay maybe a little worried, in this place it's good to know where the people are that you can trust and depend on and when you can rely on them.

It didn't take long for Frank to get back to the bunks from delivering my note. Frank pulled out a deck of cards and started shuffling. I spoke as he was shuffling, "you got my attention what are we playing?" Frank smiled, "Texas hold'em I'm told is your game."

I started to smile as I spoke, "Who have you been talking to behind my back. Look at you go Mr. Background check." Frank lightly smiled and responded, "Chap told me to keep you out of trouble for him since I seemed to follow you everywhere and in exchange he told me a few of the things you like to do."

At this point Frank seemed highly amused that he knew information that I didn't give out and knew stuff about me that I hadn't told anyone else. I didn't want to burst his bubble so I played along with his charade and sat at the table to play.

As Frank passed out the chips I spoke, "So why the interest in what I seem to like?" Frank answered a little hesitantly, "I just want to do things you like so you continue to spend time with me." I lightly chuckled as I put my chips in order and spoke, "Alright little buddy but you don't have to go out of your way. I would still spend time with you either way."

Frank smiled and we started to play. I let Frank win a few hands deliberately to keep the game interesting. I made sure I still won the game to keep his respect in check for my ability to play however. Frank seemed content that he had won a few hands and I knew I left him wanting to play again and I was satisfied with that.

Everyone was in their bunks and trying to sleep by the time we finished our game so we just shut out the lights. I had laid in my rack awake just long enough to hear the mosque music and I just put in my ear plugs and went to sleep.

4

COURAGE IS NOT THE ABSENCE OF FEAR BUT THE CONQUEST OF IT

It's been a little over a week and not much has happened besides the usual mortar attacks on the base. The patrols have had a few minor attacks but not anything special enough for Chap to care enough about to discuss with me. We had gotten our schedules down to eating lunch together almost three times a week now so I felt more comfortable about where he was and what he was doing. He seemed to be doing okay. I've been worried about Joker though he's been buried in HMMWV repairs from all the IED's. I had a patrol to go on that I was asked to help support today. Apparently there is too much mud on the base when it rains for the brass to be comfortable with so we got asked to set out patrols and set up a few positions to protect the trucks as they brought in with the gravel to cover the muddy roads on the base. All of us were wondering what the big deal was as we never had any problems with the muddy side streets on the base before. Not only do we have to do our current duties but take on these extra duties. I didn't mid the work myself but I was worried that my squad was getting burned out with all the hours we were working. I knew if I was getting tired then it was worse for them.

I had set up a few trades with the supply guys on the base. In exchange for a crate of energy drinks Chap was going to let them go on a few patrols outside the wire with his squad. I thought the trade was more than fair. Chap and I got energy drinks to last a week for everyone and the supply guys got to go off base for once and get bragging rights.

I had put Frank in charge of the sweep watch and I was taking Vince and Daniels on patrol with me. Chap had his whole squad going and there were various other teams that we spread out through the entire road.

According to the Intel for this mission we were expecting to be sniped at and attacked several times. The question was from where and when would this happen. I didn't want to focus on it to much. Makes you get all worked up on who decided to make us do such a stupid mission endangering the lives of my men just for a few rocks to go on a dirt road. I never asked questions because I know it would do no good so we have to just do what we are told. That is what is what is expected of us. However I was allowed to voice my opinion so I usually do from time to time but I had learned to pick my battles.

I was meeting up with Chap in about an hour for breakfast and then we would be heading out to our positions and patrols. Joker was already outside the wire patrolling for IED's along the route and as a side mission the guys he was with were maintaining a presence in the area to prevent anyone from placing IED's.

As I started walking to the Chow Hall Vince and Daniels came up behind me then started to fall in step to walk with me. Vince spoke and I slowed my pace, "Corporal, do you think we're going to see some action today?" I responded, "Some of us more than likely will. However I hope we don't." Daniels chimed in, "I hope we do! I need my ribbon!" Vince commented at the same time, "Yeah!" I chuckled and responded, "I'm glad you're gung ho and want some. Don't rush it it'll happen, just do your job okay?" They responded in unison, "yes corporal!"

As I got to the Chow Hall Chap was waiting at the door for me. Chap spoke as I got up to him, "You're late." I responded, "I got here when I planned to. You're early." Chap half smiled and we walked into the Chow hall.

We got in the breakfast line. It was a little longer than usual but there were a lot of people going on patrols and posts today for the gravel rock road mission. The lady at the counter started taking my order, I ordered four eggs sunny side up and hash browns fried with tomato's, mushrooms and cheese. Chap shook his head as he spoke, "You ever order anything different?" I responded, "I know what I like and I don't get tired of my favorites." Chap made his order next, an omelet with ham and cheese. The food here definitely helps my morale and I believe it makes a difference for my buddies too. I laughed and spoke, "what about you? You make fun of me and then go and do the same thing." Chap responded, "My breakfast has meat yours does not so your argument is invalid." We both gave each other a slight smile and grabbed our orders when they were done.

We went through the whole meal without speaking to each other. I didn't really have much to say myself however I could tell something was bothering Chap I figured I would pull it out of him when we got back off patrol.

When we were done eating we both left

and went our separate ways. Not sure where Chap was going to or what his schedule was but we were posted on a building along the route to look for snipers or draw fire if necessary.

I had Daniels trade weapons with Frank. I wanted to make sure we had the fire power of the M249 SAW with us while we were out. Daniels seemed to complain about how heavy the weapon and ammo were. I think it gave him more respect for Frank hauling it around everywhere though.

I wanted to get an early start so we all got into our HMMWV's and the drivers took us to our designated locations. It was a beautiful clear day and I had a good view of the Euphrates River. I was posted on a fairly remote building along the road. The back of my building was facing the river. Daniels and Vince were a little further down in another building along the road, one inside and the other on the roof.

I didn't exactly like that I was alone but there

were so many points we had to watch and not enough people to watch them. I couldn't stick the boots by themselves so I put myself here alone. I liked being alone anyway. Just not maybe when there is danger around.

I saw Chap drive by with several HMMWV's doing his rounds. Everything seemed like it was going to go nicely. The Gravel trucks were moving through pretty steadily back and forth trying to get the job done as quickly as possible.

It was over an hour before I heard the first explosion. I could see a small puff of smoke across the village along the route for the gravel trucks. There were a few shots as well but from the distance it was hard to see where it was coming from. Our communication line was different from Chaps team so I was a little worried if everything was ok. I picked up the com and told everyone on the channel to be vigilant and keep an eye out. About an hour had passed since the explosion but it seemed forever since I was waiting to see who had gotten hit but not letting myself think about it. I was relieved to see Chaps HMMWV's drive by however it was clearly evident that the third truck had been hit but it was still moving along so it was good. It was around noon and the sun was starting to beat down some hot heavy heat. The sweat was pouring from every pore on my skin and I believe I could see steam forming over my head from it!

I pulled up my binoculars to check on Daniels and Vince to see how they were doing and saw Daniels had one foot on the ledge of the roof looking through his binoculars scanning the horizon and Vince was going from window to window on the first floor making sure the building stayed clear.

As I put the binoculars down we heard a shot and our com line lit up with panicked voices. I lifted my binoculars in the direction of the shot and could see what appeared to be a water tower. Chap's HMMWV's sped past my position at a speed I didn't think the armored HMMWV's could even achieve leaving a wake of dust behind them. I had to wait until the dust cleared to see the tower again which is where they went to. As I was trying to look another HMMWV stopped and yelled for me and my squad to get in. I radioed for Daniels and Vince to join me and we sped to the Tower. When we got to the tower there were already a few marines at the top trying to get someone down. As we got closer I saw Chap yelling at a few guys to start searching houses so I yelled to Daniels and Vince to join them.

As I got to Chap he didn't give me a chance to speak first, "Sniper shot not sure if he's going to make it." I responded, "Who?" Chap answered, "Its Chris." I responded, "Shit." Just as Chap was about to respond someone from the tower yelled coming down.

As we turned to look they tossed the flack jacket down first. It was as if time had stopped and the jacket fell what felt like forever. As it hit the ground I felt my heart sink and a wave of emotions hit my face. It was as if it had drained every last bit of morale out of me.

They lowered Chris down and immediately had him in a HMMWV with the Docs working on him constantly. Just as I had a second to even process what I saw they were gone. Chaps face was drained of color and I could see the anger in his eye's.

I had hung out with Chris a few times but Chap knew Chris quite a bit better than I did and I could tell it was hitting him hard. I was about to try to say something to Chap, maybe a word of comfort or something but the com came on and we were ordered back to our posts to immediately continue the mission. The moment was gone and I was not really sure how to give comfort other than to just be there anyways, it's hard to deal with for all of us.

I got back into the HMMWV that dropped me off and we swung by where Vince and Daniels were clearing buildings and went back to our positions. I climbed back to the roof and started scouting the area with the binoculars.

A few hours went by but they were some of the slowest hours I've had in a long time. As I decided to look at Daniels and Vince to make sure they were ok I could hear Mortars landing on the Base as usual. Felt weird being on the outside seeing them land than being on the base when they were landing. The explosions actually echoed across the buildings and made it sound like more were landing than actually did. Not too long after that a fire fight started on the other side of the village. It was far enough that all we could do was watch the area it was coming from. I couldn't see what was going on but from the sounds of it. The Marines over there were laying it on thick.

I had heard it enough times I could almost play it like a movie scene in my mind what was probably happening just by listening. I had gotten a little more side tracked than I had thought. As I stood to light my cigarette and was lost in my thoughts a light whipping sound passed by and a few rounds hit the wall beside me ringing into my ears and throwing debris into the left side of my face and causing me to hit the ground.

It must have rattled Daniels and Vince to see me drop after the shot because they panicked on the radio. I couldn't quite make out what they were saying due to the ringing in my ears. I wasn't quite sure if I was ok I patted myself down to see if I was bleeding but it was just minor scrapes on the side of my face.

I must have been dazed or took longer to get up than I thought because by the time I was trying to stand up Daniels was already at my side trying to help me up. As he was picking me up a few Mortar rounds started to land close to the building and we decided to take cover inside.

As we got inside Vince spoke, "Shit Corporal you ok?" I responded, "Yeah just my fucking pride got hurt. How's my face?" Daniels laughed as he responded, "You're still ugly as ever Corporal." I laughed and responded, "Fuck you to Daniels. Alright let's re-secure the house and I will post on the roof you two watch the main floor." They both responded, "Yes corporal," then went to secure the main floor.

As I got to the roof I could see where the two mortars had landed in front of the building there was dirt debris floating around and I was now looking through a dust cloud. I was scanning the area when Chap stopped in front of the building to see if I was okay. I gave a wave and he left without getting out.

It wasn't long after that when the last of the gravel trucks finished with their loads that we saw the last one go by. We got called to load up and head back to the base. Our HMMWV came by and we gladly jumped in. Ahhh, home bitter sweet home, we went back to the bunks to unload our gear. It was time for Chow but I wasn't in the mood to eat at the moment too much was weighing on my mind. I guess some others did not feel like eating either and as we were relaxing in the racks a runner came by the bunk to let us know that Chris didn't make it.

After that I decided tonight was a good night to pull out the stash I had been keeping that I had been stocking up from the mail. I wasn't even 2 drinks in when Chap showed up, I knew in my gut he would come. He didn't talk he just took a few of the drop bottles... I had shot two back already and poured the rest into the drink he had brought.

Daniels and Vince just watched us and played cards after a while we joined in on the game. I wasn't sure what Frank was up to but by the time he finally showed up at the bunk house to join in I was too far gone to care.

After the boots took the rest of the cash I had in my pockets in the games I laid down in my bunk to pass out. As I laid there watching the room spin all I could see was the flack jacket falling. It felt like I was falling... tired, sad, and weary, I let myself fall into the darkness like the flack jacket and I wished as I fell I wouldn't get up.

5

AFTER CROSSES AND LOSSES MEN GROW HUMBLER AND WISER

A week had gone by since the gravel mission and sweep watch had temporarily been canceled for some reason so my squad and I had been doing patrols with Chap's squad in-between. I could tell it was going to be a really tough week morale wise. The service we were holding for Chris was today and I don't think anyone was going to be okay after it, we didn't have a casket or body and all we had of his was the rifle, two boots, Kevlar helmet, and a set of dog tags.

A few of his close friends had set up a video to play and a few were going to talk on Chris's behalf about the type of marine he was several times throughout the day. I wanted to do something for him as well but nothing seemed appropriate.

I left to go to the chow hall and Chap had snuck up behind me. I ignored the fact that he just dumped sand down the back of my shirt and kept walking. Chap spoke, "There's a Texas hold'em game around noon you in?"

I just kept walking for a moment longer before speaking, "Why do you want me in this game?" Chap responded, "the pot is $500. We can split it 50/50 you in or not?" I shrugged as I answered, "Sure put me in." Chap slapped me on the back and spoke, "we'll be by the quad cons with a table don't be late." Then Chap was gone as fast as he had snuck up on me.

I looked at the watch of the Army officer next to me to get the time. The watch looked nice it looked like a Rolex however I knew better. I had seen so many fake ones in the jewelry shops in Kuwait that's probably where he actually bought it.

It was 10:30 so I had plenty of time to waste

before the game. I figured I would go ahead and walk down there and take a nap; naps are always a good way to just not think. A human body can't be walking too far in this heat even if the sky was a beautiful blue with no clouds because the suns hot rays burn like lava as they roll down your uniform and skin. There is nothing like the heat to make you feel the hell of this place. Once I made it to the quad cons I sat on one of the concrete barriers that were close to them in the shade made by the camouflage netting. I propped my feet up on the barrier next to it tilted my hat down and my mind disappeared into oblivion.

I was lovingly woken up by Chap kicking my feet off the ledge and instantaneously I could see the table was all set up and the chips were passed out. I slowly and casually moved to the open chair and put my money in the hat with everyone else's for the buy in and $100 wasn't bad for a game and Chap and I had 2/5 chance of winning so I figured it was worth the gamble.

The game started and we played a few hands before it really started to get interesting. It was the ninth hand of the game and I was still about even. Chap was up by double and with what I just got dealt I had a full house.

The other marine raised the pot so I sat thinking what he could have that would beat my hand. Chap laughed and spoke, "Dude, he's bluffing go all in... I'm serious do it." I thought for a second searching in the other marines eyes for a tell but was still unsure.

Chap spoke up again, "Dude just do it." Tired of trying to figure out what tell he had I called him all in. The other marine stared at my face for almost ten minutes before deciding to go all in with me. We watched as Chap put all the chips into the middle in order before we showed our hands.

Once the chips were counted we both showed our hands at the same time. I had the full house but the other marine's full house was higher. I spoke, "Damn, Damn, Damn you Chap, Fuck you!" Chap was at this point rolling on the floor.

Once Chap was done laughing he spoke, "I can't believe you listened to me, you're such an idiot!" I responded, "Fuck off, I'm heading back to the bunks." I walked out pissed that Chap deliberately baited me and knew I was going to lose the hand. I should have listened to my instincts but I thought of us working the game as a team which would have made Chap want us both to be in. He apparently was willing to spend $100 just to get a joke on me. He sure had a good laugh at my expense, He still has a gleam of humorous fun radiating off of him the asshole. Well, at least he is still in the game... maybe he could win on his own.

I started to walk away and had just rounded the corner when I heard what almost sounded like a small rocket. Before I could turn around whatever it was exploded inside the compound I had just come out of. The explosion was big enough I could feel it's compression even on the other side of the barrier as small debris came out of the entrance way. I scrambled to see if everyone was okay. I came around the corner and could see a huge gaping hole in the quad con behind where we were playing poker.

The quad con was ripped open in jagged pieces twisting in several directions but what amazed me more than the damage was everyone was running out of the area except Chap… and me gapping at him yelling, "You leave the table you forfeit the chips you pussies!" The hole was still smoking and apparently Chap was not going anywhere until he had collected all the money and the chips from the game. I came over and helped him collect the rest. I looked at the cards scattered everywhere and spoke, "You're a piece of work you know that man?" We only snagged the chips and money as we were not playing 52 card pick up and left the premises in record speed as well.

We just started rounding the corner when the emergency response team pulled up in the HMMWV's to asses what happened. They didn't even bother talking to Chap and I, they went straight to the quad con and started grabbing certain pieces of debris off the ground. Chap and I watched them work and they didn't waste any time at all. Once they were satisfied with what they had picked up and seen they reported no casualties or injuries and one damaged quad con... then sped off as fast as they had shown up.

Chap looked at me and spoke, "Well shit, glad we are important around here and worth checking out." I responded, "Awww you want a cookie to make you feel better?" Chap gave me an evil glance and attempted to arm bar me. We hit the ground wrestling for a moment until I got the upper hand putting Chap in an ankle lock...it was a dirty move since I knew he had injured it around a year ago shooting fireworks at my grandparents' house. I mentally paused with the memory... Wow, it seems like such a long time ago, but anything goes in a tussle to win and he would have done the same to me.

Chap gave a sharp "shit" yelp and surrendered pretty fast as I gave his ankle a sharper twist for good measure. We both got up and started lightly laughing. Chap spoke as we started walking, "I'm keeping the cash you left the table." I responded, "Whatever... I only left because you egged me on and I lost." With that we both went our separate ways.

I was headed to see Chris's memorial and video, it was running several times for all the different shifts everybody had. I wasn't sure what to think going into it but I wanted to go this time. I had missed one of my best friends and still regretted it and I didn't want to do that twice. When I got to the Chapel I saw Chris's picture was on an easel in the center, next to it was his gear properly placed, at the bottom were his Boots at a perfect 45 degree angle, and the rifle was in-between with his dog tags and Kevlar helmet hanging.

I sat in the pews for a moment not sure what to think. As I sat there one of Chris's good friends came in to talk about him. He talked about how great of a friend he was and how he would be missed. He talked about how well he treated his wife and daughter... as his friend continued talking I started to remember his flack jacket falling from the sky. It was in slow motion, falling like time was almost at a stand-still. That is the strongest part of his memory for me at the moment something I couldn't seem to forget. I tried to focus on the positives his friend was talking about but I couldn't focus anymore...time seemed all out of whack.

I didn't think I was giving off any emotions sitting there but the Chaplain (who was an officer) came over and spoke, "You seem like you need an ear. Could I lend you one?" I responded, "I appreciate the thought Sir but I don't think there's anything you could help me with." The Chaplin responded, "Who said I was trying to help you with something? Sometimes you need to talk in order to help yourself. Just think on it. I'm here if you need me." The Chaplin got up and went back to the stand where Chris's picture was. I sat for the better part of an hour before I decided I had been there long enough. I walked up to the stand after Chris's friend had gone and placed my hand on the picture and left the Chapel.

I could hear Mortar rounds hitting somewhere north of me as I walked out of the Chapel and almost immediately the siren started going off. I'm not quite sure my inner timer is working right at this point because once again time seemed to slow down and all the noises around me were muffled... it was as if the world had stopped moving. I could hear a low thump as another round landed somewhere on the base. The siren sound was now deep and slower my vision almost blurry. I lifted my hands palm up level with my waist to look at them and they felt heavy and looked far away, just as fast as everything suddenly slowed down, it was back to normal. That was freaky feeling and I walked to the nearest barrier and sat down and pulled out a cigarette to smoke it. By the time my smoke was lit the siren had stopped going off. I finished off my cigarette decided that I was done for the day, I'm not even sure what the hell happened and was getting frustrated and confused just thinking about it. I decided to just let go and move on as there was nothing I could do about a time warp besides, I didn't want it affecting the rest of my tour. In the back of my mind where I shoved unwanted thoughts, hovering in the front of that space was... I just hoped it didn't happen again.

When I got back to the bunks joker was waiting on me. Joker spoke when I sat down, "How you doing?" I responded, "good... you?" Joker answered, "I don't know how I'm doing. I'm going out on EOD soon. You?" I responded, "I'm back on towers and Sweep watch."

I could tell something was bothering Joker but I couldn't place what it was enough to think of an appropriate way to get the information. So we sat there silent for a moment until Joker got up and went to the door. As Joker got to the door he turned around and spoke, "Why did you come back here?" I thought for a moment before responding, "You guys." Joker cracked a small smile but it faded away fast. Joker then left and didn't shut the door. I just sat watching it swing in the wind.

As I sat in my bunk my squad slowly came into the bunk house one at a time throughout the rest of the evening. They were laughing and joking around with each other and just enjoying not having to really do anything for the day.

I lay down in my rack to get some sleep. I had my eyes closed but I could hear every sound in the room as if I was fully awake. I could hear Vince picking on Daniels...Daniels in turn picking on Frank...the team seemed to really be getting along now. There was something about this place that no matter how bad it was or got, the people you were here with could drag you through it. I listened as I laid in silence and I could tell there was a complete difference of the squad from where it used to be to where it is now. As I thought about the bonds and relationships I started to think about the last tour and everything that had happened up to this point. How was I holding it together? Why hadn't I let go yet? Why was I still fighting?

I didn't get too much further into my ruminating questions before I fell into oblivious darkness, there were no dreams any more just darkness. I was no closer to getting my answers than I was getting a true night's sleep as only the Dark claims my mind now.

6

VICES ARE THEIR OWN PUNISHMENT

Everything seemed to get back to normal for the base after a week or so. Sweep watch started again today and we were back on tower duty for now. Chaps patrols had increased and apparently the Captain was ribbon hunting and demanding to go outside the wire where we all knew he didn't belong.

It had been a while since I had seen Omar and I was looking forward to whatever he was bringing. The mortar attacks on the base were still pretty consistent and more frequent than I remember them being from last time.

It seemed the closer to the holidays we got the worse the attacks seemed to get. Ironically I think they were attacking to drop morale for the holidays. Everyone was excited by the attacks so they had a chance to get their ribbons and get some action.

I was in the chow hall thinking about guys ribbon hunting and everything I had done up to that point when a tall gruff looking marine sat next to me. He was built pretty large and looked as if he went to the gym all day every day. I wasn't sure why he sat next to me so I didn't say anything yet and continued to finish my breakfast. I stood up to leave when I was done and he placed his hand on my shoulder and forced me back in my seat and spoke, "You can't leave yet."

A little confused, I didn't argue with the massive marine and I waited picking at the fruit I had left on my plate. This marine was obviously the muscle for whoever was coming and I racked my brain to think of why I would be wanted, I wasn't sure what I had done to gain any ones attention. I personally hadn't done anything noteworthy quite yet that I could think of. Then, I recognized the man as soon as he walked through the door… it was Youssef, I had almost forgotten about him with his wheeling and dealings. In retrospect I figured he'd be dead by now or back home.

Youssef came over to the table and sat on the other side of me and waived the other marine away. I lightly chuckled and spoke, "What can I do for you Youssef? You obviously want something from me or want me to do something." Youssef spoke, "I'll be blunt with you, you work on a detail that has certain individuals that have information I want, and they also have the best ability to smuggle in anything you like. You bring in what you want no questions asked, I get information I need, and we both leave the better for it."

I thought for a moment, he must be referring to the sweep detail. I figured out Omar was the informant for the base just recently. I could only guess at what information Youssef wanted from him.

I spoke, "if the detail doesn't want to

cooperate?" Youssef smiled and responded, "Here is a note (Youssef passed me a folded piece of paper) hand it to them to read and I'm sure they will be more than generous and cooperative."

I looked at the paper but it was all in the local language which I couldn't read. I looked at Youssef and spoke, "I'll find you when I have an answer." Youssef smiled and spoke, "you can find me near the palace most of the time by the helipad."

I got a slight rush just thinking about getting my hands on something I could use. But I was also concerned I might be jumping into a pot of boiling water. Either way I didn't have a choice. Youssef wasn't someone you messed with. Plus I could see by his muscle he had quite the pull out here now.

I left the chow hall and started heading to the sweep detail. I reached the Gate where Omar and his buddies were waiting and they happily greeted me. Omar spoke, "I have gift for you here. You want now?" I shrugged my shoulders and answered, "Sure." Omar handed me a decent sized package. When I opened it there was a bottle of jack Daniels, a Koran, and a few more pieces of jewelry. Omar shook my hand and spoke, "You like take now, two hundred dollar yours… anyone else four hundred."

I laughed slightly. Some gift if I had to pay. But I guess smuggling it in was no easy feat being nonmilitary. I spoke, "Sure two hundred tomorrow." Omar responded, "Not today?" I chuckled and answered, "I have to get the money."

Omar thought for a second and answered, "Tomorrow is okay." I put the gifts in the pack Frank was carrying and we started the daily sweep detail. It was still amazing to me we were sweeping the streets. It made for a long day and it was completely unproductive. About half way through our sweep detail a few mortar rounds started landing, I paid close attention to Omar and his buddies and there was no reaction, they didn't even flinch once. I started to think they all had probably been through quite a bit at this point.

I decided it might be a good moment to open a conversation with Omar so I spoke, "How do you feel about us being here?" Omar gave a slightly confused look before speaking, "It's safer with you here but only where you are... Where you are not, is not so safe."

I thought for a moment before speaking, "Explain where I am not." Omar had a slight frown as he spoke, "it's like this, I come here I help you, I make money, I go home... When I go home, I have lots of American cash. Other people they know this... It makes lots of opportunities for very bad things, yes?"

I responded, "So the cash you get makes you a good target for bad people. Why take the cash?" Omar smiled as he spoke, "I'm now richest person in my village. I have much respect. That gets me many things. I work on base also make me more money with someone like you who like nice things.

I give money to other families so we all can live better."

I thought for a moment on the words Omar had said. What I got is money is dangerous here but gets respect from others and makes living easy so is worth the risk of having it. Omar pulled a crumpled map out of his pocket and handed it to me.

He spoke as I looked at it, "I make big deal with you. I offer others but no one can do yet. My house here (Omar pointed at a spot on the map north of the Euphrates river) you patrol make village safe. I give you anything you ask."

I smiled as I had gotten to the part of the conversation I was waiting on and spoke, "All I need is for you to give someone some information." Omar smiled and spoke, "I already give your other guys information this is easy you want more?"

I laughed and spoke, "I do but I will pay for what I want this information will have no money with it." Omar shook his head in agreement and spoke, "You patrol first and information is yours." I shook his hand and we carried on with the sweep detail.

The rest of the day dragged on and it felt like forever for the sweep detail to be over. Almost at the end of our unproductive duty I told frank to put my "supplies" in my bag back at the bunk house. He didn't say anything and took off.

As Omar was setting down the broom and getting his stuff together to leave he looked at me and spoke, "You no forget money tomorrow and make home safe." I didn't respond and just gave him thumbs up as I got him to sign his hours and I left back to go back to the other side of the base.

I would have to find Chap and see what I could do about the patrols but first I needed to go to the ATM by the USO to get the cash I owed Omar for tomorrow. As I was coming up to the USO there was an Army Soldier showing off to a few Marines. I couldn't tell what style of martial arts it was but it was a little impressive with how high he was kicking, I had heard a few stories about him before but this was the first time I had seen him in action. I wondered if he was trying to impress someone enough to take him on patrols or something similar, why else would he be showing off I figured.

I slightly chuckled as I continued past and walked into the USO. I was low on smokes so I bought some and I got a roll of dip cans for Chap. I had noticed he had been dipping more the last time I saw him. As I got my bags and took the cash from the ATM on my way out I watched the Army soldier for a moment again then continued to the bunk house.

Once at the bunk house I set everything in the places I had for them and checked my bag for my stuff Omar gave me this morning. It was all there so I pulled it out and put the bottle of Jack Daniels in my pillow case and placed the Koran on the shelf above my bunk.

I figured Chap should be done with whatever he had been doing all day so I set out to find him. I looked in his bunk house and saw some of his squad but not Chap so I left to wander the base hoping I would run into him. After walking a while and checking a few places I finally found Chap in the Motor pool with Joker. Both were sitting and smoking as I came up, Chap spoke as I got closer to them, "What is your punk ass up to bro?" I responded, "Looking for your dumb ass."

Chap flicked his mostly smoked cigarette at me and stood up then spoke, "You only look for me if you're in trouble or are trying to make trouble which is it?" I smiled as I spoke, "Maybe getting into it, still not clear on the number of problems I might have."

Chap chuckled then spoke, "What can I do ya' for?" I smiled and responded, "I need an adjusted Patrol route temporarily." Chap looked slightly confused and spoke, "What do you mean adjusted and how temporary?" I smiled again and answered, "I need a village patrolled a few times to make a few people feel safe."

Chap laughed and responded, "That's it? What's the catch?" I responded, "No catch but I got a bottle of Jack to share in exchange, what do you say?" Chap and Joker both smiled and both punched me in the shoulders then chap spoke, "how'd you score that and what are you into?"

I smiled and spoke, "My little Sweep detail seems to be very resourceful, likes cash and safety. All of which we can provide." Chap laughed and spoke, "Awesome, it's done. That's too easy bro." I smiled and spoke, "good, here's the map of his area (I handed Chap the map). I'm not sure who all is in the area I guess just patrol around the section marked."

Chap put the map in his pocket and spoke, "Speaking of patrols. I've got a hilarious story for you. You know that Captain Greg has been going on patrols with us right?" I laughed as I answered, "yea, what a POG (that is a military insult), what happened?"

Chap began to Chuckle as he told the story, "So we're midway through a foot patrol and all of us are jumping the shit creek (a ravine that crap literally runs down like sewage) and Captain Greg goes to jump and loses his footing and lands right in the middle of it. All of us were laughing too hard to help him up as he was flailing like a helpless turtle on his back before finally rolling over to get up."

I started laughing so hard I had to sit down before talking, "so he was covered in shit huh?" Chap answered, "Dude we made him walk down wind at the very back of the patrol it was so bad." I laughed and spoke, "So he's good ol' Captain Shit now, holy crap this is never going away!"

Joker was just smiling as he smoked he obviously had heard the story already. I spoke, So Joker what about you? Any funny stories I'm missing out on?" Joker chucked before speaking, "nothing worth mentioning at the moment. You guys seem to keep entertained enough for all of us and then some." We all were lightly laughing and just sat and smoked the rest of the time not talking. An hour or more must have gone buy with us just sitting there. I didn't realize how long it had been until I started to get hungry.

I gave a false salute as a farewell to Chap and Joker as I headed to the Chow Hall. I figured since they weren't following that they had other plans for later. I didn't mind being on my own anyway. I think I've started to prefer to be alone most of the time anyway.

Chow was always good if you were getting depressed, it is the place to go for a little pick me up. It was the first time I however was eating in the Chow hall when mortar rounds started landing. It actually gave me an uneasy feeling being in a building when they were landing. I preferred to be out in the open when it was happening.

I started to think about Omar and all the

pieces I had in place and what moves I was going to make. Politics was like playing chess. You had to have the right pieces in the right places in order to keep the king from being in check. I however never wanted to lose a piece I was playing with in real life or Chess itself.

I thought of a few gifts I might smuggle in I could take back home but I don't think I was going to do too much. There was nothing at the moment I really wanted. I had my alcohol mailed to me this deployment so I didn't need to acquire any and it was nice to have it in a real bottle. I was feeling antisocial and still depressed so either way it didn't really matter right now. I needed to give Youssef something to get rid of him so I could go back to what I was doing and this at the moment wasn't much but if I got caught up in getting things again I might ruffle the wrong feathers and I didn't like how that went last time.

After I finished ruminating while eating I headed back to the bunk house and when I walked in Frank was eagerly waiting for my return. I guess he thought we were digging into that bottle of Jack. I had no intentions of opening the bottle yet and if I did it would be to celebrate something and I would need Chap here as I owed him half the bottle.

I spoke as I sat down in my fold out chair, "You look like you're waiting on some grand event what's up?" Frank responded, "Nothing Corporal, Just waiting on something to happen I guess." I laughed and spoke, "something like what?" Frank responded, "I don't know to be honest just something."

I laughed as I pulled a few of my drinks out I had gotten in the mail. I guess my buddies back home didn't clean out the food coloring droppers all the way. Some of the Jim beam droppers were still red, green and blue. I figured it might make drinking them more entertaining if it dyed our tongues though. Frank took a blue one and sure enough his tongue was slightly blue from the dye left over. I chuckled to myself and picked one with less color in it and shot it back. Hart, Daniels, Jarred, and Vince came in one after the other and started joining in.

They passed around the cards and started playing Texas Hold'em. I was awake for most of the game but the more shots I took the more tired I got. I decided to call it a night and I attempted to go to sleep.

I'm not sure how long I was asleep, maybe two hours or so before I could feel like something was nudging my hand. I thought it might be some one playing a prank. So I moved my hand fast to grab what it was. I almost flipped out when what I grabbed slightly squished in my hand and started squealing. I quickly launched it across the room and into the far wall not knowing what it was yet. The rest of the squad was quick to get up unsure at first what was going on.

When Vince turned on the lights Hart yelled out "O shit!" and pointed to what looked like a huge Rat that scampered out the space by the air-conditioner. I looked at my hand to make sure the damn thing didn't bite me and it just looked like I got a few scratches.

Daniels looked at me and spoke, "Damn corporal, that's fucked up." I responded, "You're telling me I touched the damn thing. Hope I don't get a disease or some shit. I'll fucking kill the thing next time!" The guys laughed and lay back down after Frank turned the lights off again.

I'm not sure if it was the mosque prayer music playing or because my adrenaline was up maybe both. I couldn't seem to settle down and go to sleep so I tried to bore myself counting repetitively in my mind, after what felt like an hour or so I fell into darkness.

7

YOU CAN'T SUCCEED UNTIL YOU KNOW YOURSELF INSIDE OUT

It had been uneventful for almost a week and Chap had started doing patrols around Omar's house, Omar was happy. I hadn't been able to find Youssef yet so not sure where that was going. Omar kept trying to bring more jewelry but I didn't want any more I had bought enough.

Shifts were changing soon so this week was the last week on the towers for my squad. We maintained the Sweep detail. Not sure why that hadn't switched yet. I'm assuming Youssef was the one responsible for that, possibly why I don't know as I hadn't found him yet.

I had been sitting in the Chow hall for a

while thinking about everything. I hadn't even touched the fruit I grabbed for breakfast yet. My oranges were already pealed. I had stripped my apples of their skin and started cutting them into slices.

I was on the last apple when someone sat next to me, when I looked over it was Youssef. Youssef grabbed a few slices of the apple off my plate and spoke, "So can I talk to him this morning?" I responded, "Yeah come with me to the gate. Shouldn't be a problem its secluded and I did what he wanted." Youssef smiled after swallowing the slices he shoved in his mouth and spoke, "Good now quit playing with your food so we can go then." I looked at my new watch I had gotten from Omar and responded, "We still have ten minutes calm down." Youssef looked at my watch and spoke, "Fowlex?" I responded, "Omar says it's a real Rolex I'm not sure it looks real, either way it's a damn nice watch for fifty bucks." Youssef inspected closer and spoke, "Damn good deal if it's real, looks real but can't be sure here."

I finished up the rest of the fruit and we headed out of the Chow Hall. As we came outside that same show off Army soldier was doing martial arts for some newer marines on base. It was starting to get annoying and was pissing me off, apparently I wasn't the only one he was making angry. Youssef walked over to him and started talking to him, "Dude enough is enough. We get it you know Kung Fu now go find something to do or go show off at the Gym with the Grunts."

The Army Soldier spoke, "Chillax yo, we're all friends here and I'm just doing my thang." Youssef frowned and got in his face then spoke, "go do your Thang somewhere else. You look like a retard out in the open show boating and are an embarrassment to your uniform."

The Army soldier got in a fighting stance as he spoke, "You going to stop me chicken shit?" Youssef smiled and spoke, "Why not." Youssef and the army soldier now were in a fighting stance and the surrounding spectators made a circle around them.

The Army soldier moved in and took a few swings and Youssef dodged them then backed up. Youssef started waving his arms in the air and making random crazy loud noises. At first I was confused and had no clue what Youssef was doing. It must have confused the Army soldier as well because when his guard dropped with a befuddled look Youssef decked him square in the throat. The Army soldier dropped immediately gagging and coughing and Youssef pushed a few people out of his way as he left the circle.

Youssef looked at me and spoke as we walked, "Never under estimate misdirection and random action. It will always confuse a too serious opponent." I lightly laughed as I responded, "Well I'm glad someone hit him. I think he was getting on everyone's nerves what a fucking POG."

We continued to the gate and I greeted the Sweep detail. I told Frank and Daniels to go ahead and start with the others. I spoke and waved Omar over as he started to go, "Omar over here for a bit." Omar looked confused and spoke, "No sweep today?" I responded, "Not yet, information first," Omar smiled and spoke, "Yes information for you sure. My house very safe now, thank you!" Youssef started speaking, "A month ago you were seen going to Baghdad with a lot of American money. We have pictures of the men you were dealing with.

Youssef pulled out the pictures in his pocket and handed them to Omar. Omar looked at the picture for a moment and spoke, "What you want to know?" Youssef slightly smiled in what looked sinister, "I need to know where these two men are staying at (Youssef pointed at two of the pictures)."

Omar looked slightly ghostly as if the color was draining from his dark tanned face. Omar swallowed hard and spoke, "These bad men very bad men. Money is for my family's safety. I pay and they stay away. They no like people how you say... nosing around."

Youssef spoke again, "You promised information and this is what I require Omar." I could see Omar's hands were trembling as he spoke, "for this I need more. Very dangerous what you ask." Youssef spoke, what's your price?" Omar answered, "My family go states be safe. No more here, we go."

Youssef thought for a moment and spoke, "Okay Omar you get me this information and I will do that for you." I could only think of how many ways Youssef wasn't going to do that. I wasn't sure if he was lying or telling the truth.

Omar stuck his hand out in agreement and Youssef shook it then Omar spoke, "Give me time, I do this for you." Youssef spoke, "Excellent you guys have an awesome day!" Just as if nothing had gone on Youssef left.

Omar and I caught up with the sweep detail and acted like nothing went on. Frank and Daniels gave me a confused look but I waived my hand in a no motion and they got the hint that it was none of their business.

We finished up the Sweep detail on time and I had tower duty tonight so I headed back to the bunk house to get my gear ready. As I was coming back from the bunk house to go to the chow hall I could hear a commotion on one of the radio's in a nearby building.

It sounded like a fire fight was going on somewhere off base I could vaguely hear it so I wasn't sure who it was or where it was. It was over by the time I got closer and could hear clearly. I continued to the chow hall and got a laugh as two Officer female soldiers hit the dirt as mortars started raining on the base as per usual.

All I could think was how funny their faces looked as they hit the dirt. What made it funnier was the fact they were officers. Not sure what unit they were from I wasn't familiar with their badges, I had checked them myself and continued on my way.

When I got to the Chow hall an Ambulance HMMWV went speeding by. I figured it must have one or two people from the fire fight in it. I didn't bother wondering who it might have been. There was no changing what was going to happen so I continued to go get my food.

The Chow hall was emptier than usual. I had a feeling of relaxation. I think I liked it better this way. I looked at my watch and noted the time. I would definitely attempt this time again to see if it was like this every day and just as I sat down with my plate of food, a flood of people started coming in. Well, there went that nice feeling... it was gone as quick as it came. I heard a shout from behind me as I picked up my fork, "Hey! Don't eat so fast let me get my food I'll join ya!"

I turned around and saw Chap in the lineup that just came in. It didn't take more than ten minutes for him to get through the line and sit at the table with me. As usual his plate had nothing but Meat and Cheese on it.

Chap didn't even get a second bite into his food before he started talking, "Dude, you wouldn't believe how my day went." So we start patrol this morning with Captain Shit pants, Oh that's his new nick name by the way." Chap took another bite of food and continued, "Not only do we almost lose him today because he couldn't keep up with the patrol, but he calls into the com where everyone with a radio can hear him and begs us to slow down."

Chap took some more food in his mouth then continued, "Then not even 20 minutes ago we get into a light engagement with some fucking insurgents. Don't know if you know the guy, Sergeant Jade, which by the way I'm glad it was him, the fucking shit head, I hope he dies, gets shot in the side."

Chap swallowed the rest of his food and shoved more in continuing to talk, "Captain Shit pants does exactly that he shits his pants running like a fucking pussy as the rounds are flying. Needless to say we have to take care of the whole thing on our own as our fearless leader is huddled on the ground in a fetal position like a whiny bitch."

Chap shoveled the rest of his food in cleaning his plate and continued talking, "So that's how my fucking day went, fucking wonderful with plenty of fucks given to everyone.(Chap swallowed his food in-between breathing and talking). So how's your day going?"

I lightly chuckled as I spoke, "well I'm glad you are okay. As for my day pretty uneventful, played politics and found out Youssef is hunting key terrorist targets in the area you know the usual." Chap frowned as he spoke, "I hate Youssef more than captain shit pants or sergeant piss head. You get this over with and done and cut ties with him soon.

I smiled and spoke, "I will I promise. I'm keeping my head down. We did enough poking around last time." Chap still wasn't smiling as he spoke, "Damn right you did and you're doing it again. Stop this shit and mind your own business. Quit getting involved in something that doesn't and shouldn't involve you."

I stood up and patted Chap on the back as I

spoke, "relax buddy nothing is going to happen to me. Just make sure nothing happens to you." Chap still didn't look impressed as he spoke, "If something happens to you I'll have to do something about it that's what I'm worried about don't be a dumb ass."

I left Chap at the table. I could see he went up to get seconds. I was full and needed to get to the main gate for tower duty. Every one that was in the chow hall were all telling the same stories as Chap and all laughing about it. I figured it was going to take a while for the Captains story to go away, he was getting pretty infamous on base.

I got to the main gate. Daniels, Vince, Frank, And Hart were all waiting on me. They had all their gear ready to go. I could see their packs were full of energy drinks. We all sat smoking for about ten minutes as we waited for it to be time for us to go up and replace the current watch.

I stood up as we had two minutes left and spoke, "okay boys lets go to the towers and give me a com check when you get there. I walked into the bottom of the tower and relieved the corporal on duty. I set up my stuff and waited on com checks.

It didn't take long for every one to check in. I wrote in the log book the time and dates of the log checks and just sat there waiting for something to happen. Tower duty at night tended to be long and tedious and it always felt like it lasted forever. Plus with doing things all day and not getting a chance to sleep prior to it always made it hard to stay awake.

It had gotten dark out now and you could clearly see the twinkling stars in the night sky. Just as I began to enjoy the peaceful feeling, a few panicked voices came over the com, "We're getting lasered! We're getting lasered! There's a sniper out here!" I picked up the com and spoke, "Calm down tower. What is your number?" The tower responded, "This is tower six and there's a laser on us!"

I had to stop laughing before I radioed the

tower again, "Tower six this is com one, which direction is the laser coming from?" The tower radioed back, "I don't know west maybe it's gone." I responded tower that is inside the base do you want to correct your direction?"

At this point I could hear other people laughing at tower six due to the fact they just got pranked again. I had a good idea of who was doing it but I just hadn't seen them doing it. I would confront them about it later until then I just sat in my chair laughing waiting on tower six to radio me back. After a few minutes tower six radioed back in, "Com one this is tower six after thinking a bit I think it was coming from the river. Is anyone else getting lasered or just me?" I responded, tower six, this is the seventh time you have been lasered on shift are you hallucinating? I'm sending the corpsman on duty to check on you."

The Doc on duty gave me a funny look and I spoke, "What... can't a guy have a laugh, you know it's funny. Tower six radioed back, "No need com one I am fine." I responded, "Roger that tower six com one out." The doc had a smirk on his face he thought it was funny too, I guess just not as funny as I found it.

After ten hours on post my squad and I got relieved. They hurried back to the bunks to get some sleep. I didn't even bother taking the almost twenty minutes it was going to take me to get to the bunk only to have to turn around and walk back here in the morning for sweep duty.

I laid down in the corner of the room and tucked my chin down into my flack jacket and tried to go to sleep. I had skipped the last two energy drinks so it didn't take long for me to fall into darkness.

8

SILENCE IS GOLDEN AND ACTIONS ARE LOUDER THAN WORDS

The weeks seemed to be flying by. Sargent Jade survived his wounds and was sent back home. Captain Shit pants was no longer the talk of the base but was still an embarrassment to our unit. I had been doing patrols with my squad for a couple of days.

They seemed to be getting used to it. I started them light with short patrols and we had been working toward going longer and longer. Same of them were carrying up to 90 lbs. of just gear. That didn't include food or water. So I didn't want to burn them out or injure them by pushing too fast.

Chap stayed on patrols but was moved to a different area. Joker was also on patrols now driving HMMV's. Not a whole lot had been going on. I hadn't called home in a while we seemed to be fairly busy and I just couldn't seem to find the time or energy to call.

I was meeting with joker during lunch to discuss our next patrol. He was supposed to be driving me and not sure who the other drivers were that he was with. It was nice to work with him again. I hadn't seen him most of the deployment aside from the odd time here or there.

As I tried to finish my breakfast Chap surprised me from behind with a smack to the head then spoke, "You talk to Joker yet?" I responded, "No fuck face I told you yesterday I was going to sit down at lunch with him." Chap responded, "Well, fuck you too. You're having lunch dates without me, I see how it is. You know I'm on patrol then."

I laughed and responded, "Get over it. That's what worked for joker so that's what we're doing." Chap grabbed some of the sandwich meat I had on my plate and spoke,

"Fine, I got to run, I'm already behind, kick Joker in the nuts for me, later...", and Chap took off as quick as he came in.

I mumbled to myself, "Ass hole, always taking food off my plate." I finished what was left of my breakfast and left the chow hall.

It didn't take me long to get to the front gate today not quite sure why I was in such a hurry as sweep detail was going to be short. I had to leave midway to talk to Joker then catch up when we were done talking.

After waiting for about twenty minutes the sweep detail showed up and so did the rest of my squad. As Omar came up to me he waived me over to the corner of the gate entrance and spoke, "I have paper here for your friend, this is your information...you give I do no more."

I nodded my head in agreement and Omar spoke again, "You keep patrol my house it no longer safe, my family leave soon yes?" I responded, "I will talk to Youssef I don't know when you leave maybe soon."

Omar looked concerned and spoke again, "I can no longer go to city not safe, I have to leave soon, you tell him this." I responded, "Okay Omar, I will tell him." I looked at the folded letter he gave me. Whatever was written on it must have taken a lot of effort to get.

We started the sweep detail and about an hour into it mortars started landing on the base again. The sirens went off as usual. But this time more mortars started landing after the siren. All I could think was that was unusual they usually only hit twice at most. I think I counted at least six rounds two of which were bigger than usual.

After the mortars had landed there was a lot of commotion on the base with vehicles driving back and forth along the path. The sweep detail couldn't sweep with the chaos so we just continued walking at a slow pace. I checked my watch and it was time to meet Joker.

I told Daniels he was in charge of the detail until I got back and I left for the chow hall. I was walking fairly briskly because I figured Joker was already waiting on me to get there and sure enough, when I got to the doors he was just inside waiting.

I spoke as I walked in, "My bad bro. The commotion distracted me and I lost track of time." Joker responded, "Don't worry about it. It's not like I have something important to do like a fleet check before we leave or anything." I responded, "Fuck man I'm sorry."

Joker smiled and spoke as he patted me on the back, "Relax bud I'm just knocking your jaws. The fleet checks have been done already." I smiled back and spoke, "You're a dick." Joker smiled and punched my shoulder as he said, "Only to my friends."

I spoke as Joker was grabbing his lunch from the buffet, "I need four drivers for a patrol a little outside the area we are supposed to be in." Joker gave me a confused look and spoke, "for?" I answered, "We're patrolling around an informants house and the surrounding area. But I have information that he has given me that possibly has caused that area to temporarily be dangerous now."

Joker responded, "How dangerous?" I answered, "light firefight maybe an IED or two I'm not sure but according to this paper (I unfolded it and pointed at the drawings and figures). This house here has four insurgents one being a sniper that's been in this area for a while."

Joker looked closer and paused before speaking, "you think they are actually there?" I responded, "Only one way to find out." Joker gave me back the paper and spoke, "Done, I'll get the drivers and meet you with Chap." I gave Joker a thumbs up and took off back to the sweep detail.

It didn't take long to catch up with the sweep detail. They still weren't sweeping and a lot of vehicles were still on the road. I figured something must be going on off base as well to cause this much of a commotion.

We got to the end of the route and said goodbye to Omar and his buddies and headed back to the bunks to get ready for our afternoon patrol. When we got to the bunk house I spoke, "Frank wake me up when it's time to go." Frank responded, "Yes Corporal." I then lay down and took a nap.

It didn't feel like I had napped too long before Frank was calling me to get up, "Corporal it's time to get ready, We have ten minutes." I sat up and threw my camel pack on and grabbed my rifle and headed outside.

When I got to the HMMWV's I noticed that Joker had everything already loaded and ready to go. I could see the drivers he picked were all PFC's. There was Joker as the lead and he brought Brown, James, and Kelly to drive the other three HMMWV's.

We loaded up and the convoy took off to meet Chaps team which for some reason still hadn't come back on base yet. There was still day light left and the sky line was a bright orange hue as the sun was hitting the clouds on the horizon. It didn't take the convoy long to get to Chaps position. As the convoy stopped I quickly jumped out to talk to Chap and get a rundown of what was going on. I could have asked over the com but wasn't sure if the situation was too sensitive.

Chap was crouched down scanning and as I crouched next to him he said, "We located the house the insurgents are operating out of for the mortar attacks from earlier today. We've been camping out trying to confirm that there are no civilians in the home before we call in an artillery strike or we go in ourselves."

I looked at the house and I could see several men in the building but no women and children. I spoke, "how many inside?" Chap responded, "I counted eight several times and it hasn't changed so I think we are green. We've been out here the whole time waiting for a good moment."

I looked at the house one last time and spoke, "I could pull the convoy around to the back and flush them out into your direction." Chap thought for a moment and said, "Fine but only if I don't get approval for artillery."

I headed back to the convoy and relayed over the com that we were to wait for the go and then we would attempt to flush out the building. After about fifteen minutes Chap came over the com, "Convoy Alpha Dog this is Patrol Golden Eagle. First off I would like to state for the record your name is gay, secondly, stand by for incoming artillery."

We didn't have to wait long before three artillery rounds landed almost dead center of the building. As the rounds impacted and exploded it was as if the building caved in on itself then blew out in all directions as the 155mm HE rounds did their designed job of complete annihilation of the target.

Even being a distance away I could feel the compression in my chest from inside the HMMWV. I wondered how loud it was and how it felt to Chaps team being so close to the target. Chaps team moved into the rubble almost immediately scanning to see if anything was left.

Once Chaps team decided there was nothing remaining of the targets they got onto our convoy and we headed to the next patrol destination. I was a little concerned that the shelling of the house more than likely alerted the entire area we were out but we were here to clear everything so it would only speed up the process.

I just liked having the element of surprise on my side I didn't like it if someone knew I was coming, they can plan and make problems if they know we are on the move. Either way the bad guys needed to be gotten out of the area. Plus, I felt bad for Omar and his family, they were placed in harms' way just for telling us where the bad people were.

Chaps squad got out at the north side of the village I had relayed over the com on the way here where the marked house was located. The convoy then took us to Omar's house where my squad was going to start clearing and we would meet Chaps squad surrounding the target house.

As I went to step out Joker spoke, "I got a bad feeling man, be careful something just doesn't feel right." I smiled and responded, "Don't worry bro I can handle myself. You watch yourself on the roads and keep your gunner awake." Joker flipped me the bird and the convoy drove off.

As we got to Omar's house I banged on the door and announced our entry, "Omar we're coming in... make sure everyone is on the floor!" I repeated myself a second time waiting for a response, still no answer. I gave a hand signal to my squad indicating possible hostile intent and we lined up beside the door. I gave the signal and my squad kicked the door in and started clearing the house. The main floor was clear so we proceeded to clear the upstairs. I took the lead up the stairs looking for Omar with Daniels while Frank, Hart and Vince watched the main floor.

As Daniels and I cleared the rooms we got

to the end of the hall way and I could see blood on the floor. I quickly kicked in the door ignoring the bodies on the floor as I cleared the room with Daniels. When we found no hostiles we announced that the top floor was all clear.

I sent Daniels to clear the roof and scan the other roof tops and I sat on the bed looking at Omar and his family on the floor. I moved to flip who I thought Omar was over, his face wasn't recognizable however he was wearing the same clothes I had seen him in this morning and I could recognized his hands from all the greets we had every morning. I could tell whoever did this beat his skull in with the butt of a rifle, more than likely an ak47.

I paged over the com confirming I had located Omar and he was deceased. I looked at his family and had a sick feeling in my stomach. I couldn't help but feel partially responsible for what had happened however I knew the information he gave me would save multiple lives of many people I knew by eliminating the insurgents in the area.

I started moving his family close together. I took his daughters broken arms and legs straightened then out and tried to make her look peaceful after doing the best I could in my mind to honor them, I put the sheets of the bed over their bodies and went down stairs.

I tried to hold in my anger but from the faces of my squad some of it must have been coming through. I realized I had tears coming out of my eyes and that was probably why they were starring. I brushed the feelings off and gave the hand signal to move out.

We cleared most of the buildings fairly fast as no one gave resistance and everyone stayed on the floor like they were supposed to do. At the pace we were going, we would be at the target house within the next thirty minutes or so.

The remaining houses were cleared and

we waited in position at the last house for Chaps squad to get into place on the other side of the target house. We didn't have to wait long he had a few more houses to clear on his side than we did.

As Chaps squad got into place my squad covered the back for anyone trying to get out. I could hear Chaps squad enter the building as they yelled for people to get on the floor. We could hear some movement upstairs so I called it on the com for Chaps squad to hear.

There were a few shots fired as chaps squad entered on the second floor and then a grenade went off as they were clearing one of the rooms upstairs. Chaps squad was extremely fast and efficient. It didn't take them long at all to finish securing the house.

Once the building was secure Joker pulled up to the buildings and we loaded the detainee's into the HMMWV's. We all had enough for one night and headed back to base. The ride back was quiet and the night sky was clear and full of stars now.

When we got back to base we took the detainee's to the holding area for processing and to be sent to interrogation. Joker gave me a pat on the back and spoke, "I think tonight's a good night to use half of that bottle I heard you guys had a hard time."

I started to slightly smile as I looked at Joker and spoke, "appreciate the company for sure see you at my bunk house." I headed out with my squad to debrief them and after debriefing I had to fill out several forms of paper work on the rounds fired. I had my squad sign statements of what happened then they all got sent in to the command office to be processed.

By the time I got to my bunk house Joker and Chap already had a game of Texas hold'em going. I sat at the table and poured some of the Jack Daniels into my empty canteen. The guy's in the room raised their glasses to me and I did the same to them and we all shot our drinks back.

After an hour of playing poker and drinking

some of the Jack Daniels I decided I was done with the night and lay in the bunk to sleep. It didn't take long for darkness to fold over my mind as I had numbed it well from drinking a fair amount on a light stomach.

9

LET SLIP THE DOGS OF WAR

My ears are ringing, not sure what's going on. I can feel pain all over. I try to move but I'm secured down. My visions blurry but it feels as if I'm upside down. I start patting my sides and I can feel the latch for my seat belt.

As I click the release I slam into the roof of the vehicle. I must have landed on someone. As I feel around trying to get out I can feel the wet slick of blood under my hands. Not my blood... whose? We must have been on a convoy. I panic why can't I remember? I need to see. We have to secure the area. The ringing is getting lower I can hear gun fire. I think the vehicle is on fire as well I can see flashes of light like flames and I'm burning up. All I can think is...I need to see now!

I start scrambling if I could just get outside it should help. I can see blurs my sight is starting to come back. I've got to get out of this damn vehicle. I can't get the door open there's no movement inside but me. I start to wonder if everyone is dead.

I start to go into a rage. I need to get out I need to help in the fight. I start to yell and scream at the top of my lungs for someone outside to get me out of the damn vehicle. All of the sudden I can't move my arms again. Everything starts to shake.

A bright light flashes in my eyes and everything starts to clear up. I can see and everyone in the bunk house is holding me down and staring at me. I can see two of them have a bloody lip and nose as they let me go. No one says anything; they all just go back to their bunks.

I was glad the dream wasn't real but I started to wonder how long I was in the dream and how long they had to hold me down. It's not the first time my squad had to hold me down and probably wouldn't be the last.

I looked at my watch and it was five A.M. there wasn't any point in going back to sleep. By the time I calmed down enough to sleep I would have to get up anyway. It had been a long time since I had gone to confessional. I figured it would be quiet and now was as good a time as any.

It was already starting to get bright outside. You could almost forget you were in Iraq if it wasn't for all the sand. I got to the Church. Well at least as close to a church as you could get in a combat zone. As I walked in the pews were empty. It was silent and peaceful. I hadn't been in here since the funeral we held for Chris. I could see another Marine's picture was sitting on the stand that I didn't recognize. I started to wonder how many people had passed away here that I didn't know about and had worked right next to them.

I wasn't sure why I came in, to contemplate my life maybe? It just felt like the place to go when I had to think. I don't know if the chaplain didn't sleep or if he had a sixth sense when someone had been sitting in his pews.

I don't know if he recognized me from before or if he just said the same things to everyone who came in. The Chaplain spoke, "You look troubled son. Anything you care to talk about?" I just cringed some and shook my head as I spoke, "Nothing I care to share father just trying to find a little peace."

The Chaplain cracked a small smile as he spoke, "Peace is not something you are going to find here. It is within you. If you want peace you are going to have to pray and ask for forgiveness for your sins but before you do that you first have to forgive yourself."

I checked (looking inward on myself) and responded, "There is no forgiveness, out here father only death and suffering. It's not my soul that wants peace I'm already in Hell. There is no saving me father, I can only go into Hell farther taking as many Ass Holes with me as I can before I am done."

The Chaplain wasn't smiling anymore as he spoke, "There is always a way to give your soul peace. You have to want it first. Remember you came here for a reason, what that reason is seems to be what you need to find out for yourself first."

The Chaplain got up and left and I just sat there for a while thinking about what I was actually doing sitting in the pews. Once I couldn't come up with an answer I decided maybe I shouldn't have even came in the first place and left.

I walked to the Chow Hall and took my usual table close to the exit. It was fairly empty. The only thing open was the buffet. None of the cooks were there yet. I grabbed some oranges and some jello and just sat peeling all of the oranges before eating any of the food.

I could hear a light ringing noise in my ears. I had gotten accustom to it but it had been getting louder lately. It got fairly annoying when it was quiet. I tried to use my fork to pick the jello up but my hands were shaking so bad it just kept falling off the fork.

Tired of trying to eat properly I picked the jello up with my fingers and ate it as fast as I could out of frustration. I pulled the oranges into slices then ate them. My mind had been blank for the most part I had been focusing on my food but something was still tugging at me I couldn't pin point what.

It would seem I couldn't stay hidden for long as I saw Youssef walk through the door. I've learned it was never coincidence when someone I knew walked in. it was either meant to be or well planned out. In Youssef's case it was always well planned out.

I pulled out the chair next to me as Youssef came up and he sat in the chair. Youssef smiled as he looked at me and spoke, "My friend what a pleasant surprise that I find you here." I took a drink of water then spoke, "I'm not here for a social call Youssef say what you need to say and leave."

Youssef shook his finger at me and spoke; "now that's no way to treat an old friend. Are you still sore about Omar and his family? I am surprised at you. Are you going soft? My fearless compadre who charges death himself countless times."

I interrupted Youssef, "Fuck you. Just tell me what you're here for." Youssef smiled an evil grin, "there are investigators here trying to sniff a few inconsistencies out. I would hate for them to find something that would happen to label you for something that you didn't do."

I took a second to breathe before responding, "What would they perhaps find my name on that I should be worried about?" Youssef answered, "There was a certain box that was obtained quite a while ago if you recall. This box contained a few let's say less reputable items for a certain person in charge."

I frowned and spoke, "How does this involve me?" Youssef was now serious as he spoke, "I want this box in my possession so I can exchange it for some documents on a few incidents off the base. You have been trading with the locals and that documentation is among the paperwork."

I responded, "I haven't done anything illegal. Why should I care?" Youssef's tone got aggressive as he spoke again, "You should care because a few of your friends haven't been so careful in their dealings outside the base. I would hate for one of them to be pinched for something they didn't do."

I was no longer relaxed and was sitting upright and tense in my seat. I grabbed Youssef by his sleeve and pulled him in as I talked in a low and aggressive tone, "I'll get your box but if any and I mean any of my guys get pinched for something like that. You'll need more than your two meat heads here to save you from me."

Youssef smiled as I let go of his sleeve and spoke, "There's the warrior spirit I remember. Welcome back and don't disappoint me. You know where to find me when you are successful. Remember the investigators are about, don't get caught." Youssef was laughing as he left the chow hall. His goons followed shortly behind him.

I sat for a moment trying to think which one of my buddies Youssef might have something on. I couldn't think of anyone who was brining anything in. Maybe Chap was in debt gambling again. I wasn't sure I would have to poke around and find out.

On top of that I needed to find out where the box is. It must be in the office of someone important who has been here and never left and who didn't ever leave. That had to be a short list of people. On the upside I could see what was in the box this time. I had wondered last time I should have looked but didn't.

I left the Chow Hall and headed to the Motor Pool. I would need Joker to assist me with this one. He would know all the drivers and who they were driving around. I would need some assistance in tracking an officers movements and the best way to do that was through his driver.

When I got to the Motor Pool it was still early. Not too many people were around at all. Joker was reliable as ever however and he was buried in the hood of a HMMWV as I figured he would be. I don't think I ever saw him not working on something.

As I came up behind him he must have assumed I was one of his Motor T guys. He didn't even look up he just started barking for tools to be passed to him. I started passing Joker the various tools he asked for and put the ones back he tossed to the side out of his way.

After about fifteen minutes of grabbing and tossing tools Joker leaned out of the hood to take a break and spoke, "I thought that was you. Your hands are to clean to be one of my guys." I chuckled and responded, "Wasn't sure if you noticed or not. I figured you were busy and I would wait until you were done."

Joker laughed and responded, "I'm never done. You're here for something what is it bud?" I answered, "I need a list of your drivers and passengers, just the Officers that don't change drivers though." Joker looked confused but shrugged his shoulders and waved for me to follow him.

We got inside the motorcade office and he went through a few drawers before he got the sign out sheet he was looking for then spoke, "You can't keep it mind you but what you're looking for is in there somewhere if that's what you need. I got to get that HMMWV running in less than an hour so I won't be able to help you look through it."

With that Joker left and went back to work. I started thumbing through the lists trying to find what I was looking for. I found a lot more names I recognized from the last deployment than I thought I was going to find. I would have to search them all so I wrote them down and left back to go on patrol with Chap.

I knew my guys would cover for me on my shift so I didn't even bother going I needed to sort this out. I had a few favors owed to me by enough people that I could disappear for a while if I needed to. As I looked at the list I wrote down names. The one that bothered me the most was a Colonel I recognized from interrogations he would be the first target. My money was on him and I didn't want to search through too many people, that's how you get caught.

I decided instead of searching I would try confronting him with information to see what I could get in return. Making a colonel angry was not an option and getting caught sneaking around was even worse. I decided I would meet him on one of his patrols in the HMMWV that he was riding in today. It wouldn't take much to conveniently be his driver.

His convoy was leaving in over an hour and I would put my money on the fact Joker was working on an HMMWV for that timeline and that was one of his trucks. I couldn't involve Joker but I could tell the driver to see Joker and Joker would know to delay the driver without actually getting involved.

I waited by the gates smoking until all the HMMWV's started lining up to leave. I watched a few levels of brass go by before finally spotting the Colonel. He wasn't medal hunting so I presume he would go somewhere close to the front but not the lead vehicle.

I watched intently as everyone started loading the trucks. Once I saw that the Colonels Gear was being loaded in the third vehicle in the convoy I approached the driver and spoke, "Jericho!" Jericho responded, "Yes corporal?" I am here to relieve you of your duties. Go see Joker for your new duty for the day."

Jericho spoke in a panicked voice, "I can't Corporal you must forgive me, I'm driving the Colonel only he can relive me." Then you are taking on an extra passenger and relax you're going to make people nervous."

Jericho didn't argue with me being a passenger but I knew the Colonel was going to notice really quick something was off so I had to think fast as he came up to the door. I opened the door as I spoke, "Good morning Colonel." The Colonel didn't even acknowledge me as he got in.

I shut the door and got in the front passenger seat. The Colonel spoke in an agitated tone, "What are you doing in my vehicle Corporal?" I responded, "I'm here about your secret box sir." The Colonel sharply spoke, "What secret box don't play games with me boy. Why are you here?"

I turned around so the Colonel could see the seriousness in my face as I spoke, Investigators are searching the base as we speak you know this. I am here for your secret box acquired by myself a few months ago on a convoy with Youssef."

The Colonel Chuckled and spoke, "Jericho let this boy drive take the day off." Jericho belted out a sharp, Yes Sir!" and was gone. I slid over to the driver seat and waited for the Colonel to open conversation. I tried not to smile too much that I had achieved not only locating the right man but doing so without getting myself in a whack load of trouble.

The Colonel spoke as we started to drive, "So you're the contraband man that disappeared a few months ago. I wondered what happened to my supply of goods." I looked back and the Colonel had lit up a fat cigar from the label on the side a Monte Christo by the size a No.3. Extremely hard to come by here.

I spoke as he was puffing in on the cigar slowly, "There is no proof of contraband sir if that is what you're looking for me to say. Someone who is good does not get caught." The colonel spoke, "Then why are you here talking to me?" A few other people I let say look out for might be blamed for something they didn't do."

The Colonel smiled and spoke, "So you thought you would just meet me and I would be understanding and help you out?" I answered, No Sir. I thought I would meet you and get terms for what you would like, in exchange for what you can do for me."

The Colonel puffed a while before responding, "Boy I could have you sent to the furthest outpost and left to rot for the rest of your time in the Corps." I smiled as I spoke, "Yes you could, but you would rather have a useful pawn that can maneuver better than you."

The Colonel smiled and spoke, "I have enough pawns doing enough things for me. I get everything I want from everyone I already have. The investigators can't get me I don't have any worries from them. I'm not about to help you and have them looking in my direction either. You didn't maneuver as well as you thought you did boy." I smiled as I held my mobile radio up and spoke, "Yes I did Colonel." The Colonel frowned and spoke, "You might think you're smart now but that's going to be short lived regardless of who's on the other end of that line.

The Colonel called for the convoy to stop then smiled at me as he spoke, "No one knows you're here boy and we're a long way from base now. How long do you think it's going to take you to get back with all that gear? A day maybe two can you last that long?

My heart fell into my stomach as I realized what he was about to do to me. They were going to continue without me and I was going to be left with nothing but what I had on me. Not quite the way I planned for this to go.

As the Colonel shoved me onto the ground he took my mobile radio and examined the channel it was on then took it. He gave me one last look and spoke, "I hope your well trained marine. This is good bye." The colonel moved into the driver seat and the convoy sped off.

I guess everything can't go as planned. What the Colonel didn't know was on the other end of the radio was the investigators. I had enough info that they would go after the Colonel and leave everyone else alone for now.

I had two choices at the moment hold out where I was and hope that the investigators could figure out where I was or I could try to sneak back and avoid the investigators all together and put all this garbage behind me.

I thought for a moment and decided I would make it to the base or die trying. Joker would know I left and he would get me once he figured it out but that would be hours from now. With luck I could make it to base before dark.

After about and a few hours of trying to be sneaky I decided fuck it. If I make it good for me if not just don't get captured alive. At this point I was pretty much walking in the middle of the road in full gear smoking a cigarette.

I had caught the attention of the locals and I could see there were people following me but none of them had weapons. A few of the kids came and pretended to March in file behind me but most everyone kept their distance.

I don't think the locals knew what to think with me being out there by myself. I think they thought I was trying to be bait and there were more with me. Every house I seemed to pass it looked like the people behind me were trying to catch some one hiding in them.

It was starting to get dark. I knew it wasn't wise to be in the middle of the road any more. It was actually pretty stupid doing it earlier but I didn't really care at the moment. The walk sucked, I was hot, tired, dehydrated, and hungry.

I heard the sound of HMMWV's in the distance I crouched down and let them pass. They had search lights looking in the ditches and houses. I assume they were looking for me but I wasn't sure what group they were. I would need to make it back on my own.

The rest of the night went by and I had only seen two other convoys all which were different I knew one of them were probably either Joker or Chap but I couldn't chance it. When I got to the gate chap was at the front waiting on me.

As I came up Chap spoke, "I figured you'd come in this way. What happened?" I answered, "Things didn't go according to plan. Did Joker talk to you?" Chap shook his head as he spoke, "Yeah he got the message you gave the Colonels driver. I snuck the Mobile radio into the investigators room. It almost didn't work he was just about to leave."

Chap spoke, "How did you know you could trust the driver?" I responded, "He was too jumpy and edgy when I tried to relieve him. He feared the colonel so I knew he would be quick to turn on him." Chap smiled and patted me on the back as he spoke, "You get way to lucky some times."

I headed back to my bunk house and met with my squad. Once I filled them in they continued with their duties and I laid in my bunk to sleep as tired as I was sleep seemed to evade me for a while but I finally succumbed to the darkness.

10

WHO SAID IT WAS LUCK? SURVIVAL IS A SKILL.

The investigation on the base had been pretty tight lately. It hadn't been safe to get anything in or out of the base in a few days. I had hadn't confirmed it yet but I was pretty sure they didn't figure out I was the one that turned in the Colonel.

They had took everything out of his office and cleared out where he had been staying but they never found the black box. Youssef had disappeared for a while. I was pretty sure either he had taken the black box or the Colonel had a damn good hiding spot.

I was determined to get the black box. I had found out that what was in the black box was important to a lot of people but there were a lot of people who shouldn't have it. I needed to give the information to the investigators. But I would have to do it anonymously.

The other issue is I would have to either find the box or take it from Youssef both of which was going to be difficult. I also would have to deal with Youssef. I didn't exactly do what he wanted me to do. I got the results he wanted but not how he wanted it done.

With the Colonel taken away during the investigation Youssef was now the biggest player on the base that I would have to worry about. If I could just get him out of the way or caught I could put this mess behind me.

I headed to the Chow Hall for breakfast with all of this on my mind. I was extremely distracted to say the least as I barely noticed a mortar or two landing close to me as I walked to the Chow Hall let alone the siren as it was screaming.

I got to the chow hall and went to open the door when a cloth bag quickly covered my head. I tried to elbow the person in the face behind me but missed and there must have been someone in front of me now because I caught a good punch to the gut that nearly knocked the wind out of me.

It didn't take long for the attackers to get a choke hold on me and make me pass out at that point. I started to think of suspects as I passed out. The only thing I could come up with was Youssef and his goons.

I'm not sure how long I was out for but when I woke I was in what appeared to be an interrogation room. Suddenly I didn't think Youssef was involved anymore. A sudden dread came over me as I had no leverage for being able to get out of the mess I had gotten into.

At this point I knew the investigators had something on me or believed I had some information. The only thing I didn't know is what they had or what information that I had they wanted. I had a month left in this crap hole I didn't want to leave like this.

As I continued to think in all directions a gentleman came in wearing a well pressed and clean uniform. I looked at him and figured either a paper pusher or an interrogation breaker. He would find breaking me wouldn't happen however.

As the gentleman came up he unlocked my cuffs and sat in the chair in front of me then spoke, "Do you know why you have been brought here?" I answered, "Not exactly. The greeting party was let's say, not real friendly."

The gentleman smiled as he twirled the pen in his hand and spoke, "You have caused quite a stir for someone unimportant in this place. A Colonel is taken away, information goes missing, and informants wind up dead. Where do you fit in all of this hmm?"

I slightly smiled as I spoke, "If I was so unimportant I don't think I would be in this room. Don't insult my intelligence, say what you are here for or leave and don't be wasting our time." The gentle man cracked what could have been a smile and spoke, "pretty bold for someone in your position."

I spoke again, "I'm in no bad position with obviously no credible evidence against me or you would already be at that part of the conversation." The gentleman stood up and banged on the door and another man of similar stature came in with an envelope.

The man handed the envelope to me and left the room. The gentleman spoke, "Open it and when you're done reading then we will talk." I curiously opened the envelope and pulled out a confidential file. Several of the words and names were blacked out but I could read it well enough.

Based on the information on the envelope there was a lot more going on than even I thought possible. I don't think I was here because I was in trouble I think they were having difficulty finding the trouble and with this information I wasn't it. Why the show? Were they trying to get me to confess to having leverage to help? It wasn't necessary all they had to do was ask but then again they didn't know me and I guess they didn't want to take chances so I get it. I handed the file to the gentle man and he put it in the envelope and spoke, "so?"

I responded, "Where do I fit into all of this?" The gentleman spoke again, "We need that black box. It has a list of all the key political players in the community here. The elections are coming soon. There will be several assassination attempts, bribes, threats. We need what's in that box. We know about you and all you have done. We are not concerned with you. As I said you are unimportant in the scheme of things here. We don't care what you have been doing. What we do need is this place politically stable."

The gentleman stood up and handed me a smoke and lighter. I lit it as I thought about how I was going to do this. I took a deep puff and blew it out slowly before speaking, "Either Youssef has the black box or the Colonel has it hidden well on the base."

The gentleman spoke, "Then it is Youssef who took the box as we detained the Colonel. We found the hiding spot with a few other forbidden items. The box itself was gone. Where has Youssef gone to?"

I spoke, "knowing Youssef... probably to sell the information to the highest bidder which at this point would be one of the locals." The Gentleman gave a stern look as he spoke. I will write some orders. Take a patrol to the locations you believe him to be and find him. We need him detained so we can get who he has contacted as well.

The Gentleman left the room and didn't shut the door. I am assuming that was his way of telling me I was free to go. As I left the room it was in a section of the palace I hadn't been to. I quickly left to go find Joker I would need his help setting up a patrol.

Normally I would get Chaps help but he is already gone on patrol. I found Joker at the Motor pool as usual. Not sure what he was doing but I came up and interrupted him, "Hey man I need a favor." Joker looked annoyed as he spoke, "Dude what the heck is with these orders and why are you taking so much gear?"

I grabbed the paper Joker was waving in my face and read it then handed it back and spoke, "Okay never mind that's my favor looks like I got beat coming here and talking to you. I don't know why we need heavy fire power but better safe than sorry. How long before we're ready?"

Joker punched my arm, "You're an ass hole I had plenty to do today already, give me 30 minutes and we will be ready. What are we doing man? What am I going to tell my drivers?" I had a serious look on my face as I spoke, "This one is classified Bud no one is to know anything and anything that happens is sealed."

Joker had a slight surprised and worried look on his face and rushed to help his guys load up. I had been working on a toy for a while no one knew about. I think this mission would be a perfect time to test it. I set my small hobby into my grenade pouch and started helping load the HMMWV's.

It didn't take long for us to be ready and we set out to find Youssef. As we left the base I had everyone switch to the last channel on our radios and to look out for a lost military convoy. I had a plan but wasn't sure how it was going to work this could get ugly.

After patrolling for almost eight hours we had been to six locations I thought he would be, I was running out of targets to go to. Maybe he had new contacts or someone was contacting him as we came up to our next Target location the lead HMMWV hit an IED.

It wasn't enough to do too much damage or stop the truck but I could hear the swearing over the com from the guys inside as they radioed that they were okay. We waited for a possible ambush but no one came. Joker went to the lead vehicle and checked the damage and gave the all clear signal.

We continued to a village that we hadn't patrolled in a few months. A local politician and mosque leader ran the village and wasn't in full support of us being there so we quit patrolling. As we entered the village people were surprised and looked almost panicked something wasn't right.

That's when I saw the HMMWV's parked at the mosque. It looked like there were Mercenaries there as well in a few pickup trucks that were heavily armored. As we pulled up and parked a few of the guys went into the building and I could see locals leaving out the back. Whatever transpired was obviously concluded with our presence.

As I got out of my vehicle I spotted Youssef and grabbed my toy out of my pouch and hid it up my sleeve. Youssef came up to me and spoke, "Well now isn't this a surprise whose dick did you have to suck to move up so high in the food chain as to come after me?"

I snickered as I put my hand on his shoulder, "I didn't have to do anything to get this pleasure. It fell into my lap. You my old friend are done here lets go." Youssef spoke as he tried to jerk away, "What makes you think I'm com...." I cut his sentence short with the toy I had been working on.

It was a homemade taser. I had used 2 cameras 2 nails and a few wires with electrical tape to improve it. When he pulled away I had jammed the nails into his skin and pulled the trigger on it. I was surprised at how well it worked.

I dragged Youssef to the second HMMWV and told them to secure him. Then I phoned the interrogators at HQ for further instructions. I was told to sweep the area for insurgents and collect any evidence and to instruct the Mercenaries to leave immediately.

As I ordered everyone to spread out in squads I didn't have to talk to the mercenaries they were already leaving. We weren't allowed to go in the mosque and I was sure most of what we wanted was in there. The search of the area resulted in nothing.

When we got to Youssef's vehicle however I found the black box that had caused all of this. As I opened it to review its contents I was surprised at what I had found. Not only was it a list of names of the political parties and members in the area but money contributions, bribes, smuggling rings, officials that had been bought off, almost all of this information would ruin the elections for any of the parties that's why it was so important.

As we headed back to base I started copying as much of the information as I could as a safe guard. I wasn't sure if I could trust the interrogation team let alone anyone else. We took the long scenic route back to base to give me more time.

As we got back a few MP's were waiting for us to return. They took Youssef into custody and then escorted me back to the palace in the room I started off in with the interrogator. I sat in the chair as the Gentleman walked in.

The gentleman spoke as he sat in front of me, "Congratulations on getting not only Youssef but the black box as well. Our business here is done and you are free to go. I don't know your name and you don't know mine. A man's response to the question, did you see the camel? is, what camel? You have a pleasant flight home." With that the gentleman left and I headed back to my squad. They tried to ask where I had been. I could'nt tell them the truth so I lied and told them I just needed some space and time to myself. They seemed to buy my story and left me alone.

I was beginning to wonder where Chap had been usually he comes into the middle of what I'm doing. Now that I think about it he has been gone for at least two days, after I get some rest I'm going to go check on him.

I lay down in my bunk and tried to sleep but I started to see faces of the marines and friends I had lost. I tried to push them out of my mind and force myself to sleep but darkness didn't come for a few hours and When it did come I was relieved.

11

SAFETY IS IN THE EYE OF THE BEHOLDER.

A few weeks had gone by since the investigator took Youssef. I was glad to be rid of him. I was getting worried about Chap he had been stationed off base for a while. We were leaving in two weeks and Chap was doing dangerous long patrols.

I didn't want anything to happen to him but I knew he was probably best man for the job. I had been taking care of Joker the past two days. His crew took a hard IED blast and it rattled them up pretty good. Joker had been vomiting and dizzy and the first day he couldn't even walk on his own.

He was out on patrol with Chaps team when it happened. I wasn't sure how many he had taken as a driver I think this one made it somewhere between 6 and 10 I wasn't sure. I knew of three with me and he wasn't even with me that much.

I had another hour before I had to help him to the Chow Hall again. Maybe I would just make his plate and bring it to him I wasn't sure yet. I would talk to him first and then decide what I was going to do maybe he was feeling better, being stuck in the bunk room sucks.

Waking up Joker wasn't near as dangerous as waking Chap up, I just shook his rack and Joker spoke, "Fuck you asshole. I'm going to kick your ass." I laughed as I spoke, "Ok buddy but first we got to get you to eat breakfast." Joker responded, "I'm not hungry." I spoke, "I don't care lets go."

I helped joker out of his bunk and he leaned most his weight on me. We slowly made our way to the Chow Hall. Two marines from another company walking by saw us and helped assist Joker as we walked.

When we sat Joker at the table I thanked the other Marines for their help and they left. I grabbed Joker a random assortment of fruits, yogurt, and meat to eat. Joker spoke as I sat down, "what kind of mixed crap breakfast is this?! None of this goes together." I smiled and responded, "Eat what you want and leave the rest Ill grab more of something else when you're ready."

Joker ate the fruit and tossed the rest of his plate on top of my food as a gesture of how mad at me he was. I just chuckled to myself and took both our plates up to the plate return cart. I put more fruit and some cheese this time on Jokers plate and cheese and meat on my plate then sat back down.

Joker was usually talkative with witty comebacks and remarks. He would poke fun at me or someone else, I could tell he wasn't himself but I figured he would get over it and get back to normal soon. We all go through the same thing at one point in time you get used to it and just help each other out.

Once we were done with breakfast I took Joker back and set up his TV for him. Not sure where they scored the video game console but that would occupy him for the day until I came back to help him to dinner. One of his guys was helping him during lunch.

I went back to the bunk house where my squad was. It was our day to rest and recoup. I decided I was going to pack most of my things in preparation to leave. I would just wash my laundry more often and skip a few showers.

I started looking through all the pictures on my camera that I had bought while I was here. I had pictures of the river when I had stood post at the main gate. I took pictures of the mortar holes we randomly found around the base.

There were pictures of weapons caches that we had found that the insurgents had buried in the ground. I had some pictures of the locals. I had pictures of the people that had been killed by the insurgents. I knew they were going to make us hand the pictures over for review. They had taken everything I had last time relating to sensitive information.

I had a plan to send it out through the mail currier on a small USB. You never know when you need proof of anything you were involved in. Something the military taught me was trust only you. Even the people who would die for you in battle would steal your money or have sex with your woman given the chance.

This wasn't the case with everyone; Chap hated my taste in women for one and two I had no money for him to take. So there were always exceptions. I wouldn't trust Chap with my alcohol or my tobacco but I could trust him with anything else.

I locked up my duffle bag as I stuffed in the rest of my things I knew I wouldn't need in it. I didn't have too much to do so I relaxed until lunch. Chap was supposed to be coming by for a short time before heading outside the wire for another week.

When it was time for lunch I was woken by Chap flipping my rack and dumping me out of it. I wasn't amused but I wasn't angry either. I put my bunk back together and my stuff back on it and Chap and I headed to the Chow Hall for lunch.

We went through the lines at the buffet, Chap and I loaded up our plates and sat down at our usual table. We started eating and Chap had a funny look on his face. I spoke, "What's the matter with you?" Chap responded, "Umm nothing I hope. Let's finish eating and go. Actually... let's go now."

I spoke, "What's wrong?" Chap answered, "I just need you to follow close behind me and not say a word." I didn't question Chap any further. As Chap stood up he spoke again, "Damn. That's what I thought. Let's go quickly."

As I followed closely to Chap I could see a stain starting to come through the back of his pants. As I noticed it I closed the gap closer to keep anyone else from noticing. Chap and

I left the Chow hall and went straight to the wash rooms.

As Chap got in one of the stalls he spoke, "Go to my bunk and in my duffle bag you will find my sweat pants I will be right here waiting. I tried not to laugh as I left to go get him a change of clothes. I knew he must have been embarrassed but I didn't want to make him feel worse at the moment.

The clothes were exactly wear Chap said they would be. I grabbed them and returned to Chap. He put on his change of clothes and came out and I noticed he had ripped his name tag off his pants and had it in his hand.

Chap spoke, "Don't say a word about this ever." I responded, "It's all good bro, you're not taking your pants?" Chap answered, "Yeah... No they aren't salvageable. Trust me they can sit in the stall for someone else to throw out. Let's get out of here before someone else comes in."

Chap and I headed to his bunk and Chap

spoke as we walked, "Man that local food is killing me. I don't know what is wrong. It's been like crap through a goose for a few weeks now." I just chuckled. Chap spoke again, "it's not funny. I'm serious."

After a few moments of silence Chap spoke again, "I don't have too much time to spare. I have to head out again soon so I better change... again." I responded, "Alright bro. I'll sees you when you get back so we can head home. I'm ready to leave and eat fast food again."

Chap went into his bunk house and I continued to walk around the base. I wasn't far into my walk when I could see another group of marines coming fresh onto the base. As they drove by it wasn't hard to tell that a lot of them were boots.

I wondered who they were coming in to replace. Our replacements weren't here for another week. I continued down the streets of the base just observing my surroundings. I knew I wasn't going to miss this place.

I began to wonder if I was ready to go back home. I didn't exactly do well when we got home last time. I would need to be more diligent in keeping myself busy I think. Maybe if I planned it out now and kept a schedule it would be different this time.

I continued to walk around until it had gotten close to time for dinner I still needed to assist Joker. They wanted him back on shift tomorrow but I wasn't sure how he was going to do it. Knowing Joker he would work through it even if he wasn't ready.

I headed toward Jokers bunk house and by the time I got to his bunk house it was time to eat. I was already starving I only ate a few bites of lunch before "the incident". I started to chuckle to myself thinking of Chap again. I thought about a few good jokes about him being full of shit and I would have to remember them for later.

I walked into Jokers bunk house and he was playing video games. I could see he had some Motrin out someone must have gotten it for him. I don't know if the Doc thought he was exaggerating his symptoms or not but Joker should have had a lot more than Motrin but Doc is Doc and you can't argue with what they give.

Joker was able to support most of his weight now and just needed a little assistance. I figured he would be good for tomorrow so I wouldn't worry about it. I think Joker was taking not being able to work hard as well and he wanted to go back to work anyways so I left the subject alone.

I tried to think of a subject to cheer him up. When I came up with something while we walked I spoke, "Ready to go home?" Joker slightly smiled and responded, "Yeah. This place blows donkey balls, and I miss my family."

I responded, "Yeah me too. I think we've had enough of this crap for a while." I could see Joker was starting to lighten up a bit as we continued to walk to the Chow Hall. It was good to see him feeling better.

As we sat in the Chow hall eating a few mortars started landing and I could see Joker slightly twitch. I recognized the symptoms only because I tried so hard to hide it in myself. I thought about saying something but as the siren came on I just kept eating.

We sat in silence as we continued to eat our food. Once we were done eating I noticed almost an hour had gone by. Joker and I left the Chow Hall and went back to his Bunk House and once I was content Joker was feeling alright I left and headed to mine.

When I got to my Bunk House my squad was already playing poker and having a good time without me. It made me smile to see how well they were doing together versus how it started when we got here.

One thing I will say about this hell hole is it bonds people in a way I've never experience before. That was the only positive thing I could think of about this place. The weather sucked. It would be horrible living here. Disease and starvation were common. I couldn't imagine being raised here let alone trying to have a family here.

I just sat on my bunk watching my squad enjoying not having to be somewhere or worry about something. All I could think was this was almost over. Soon I would be home. Then not long after that I would be out of the Marine Corps. I would be free.

I had done my time. I had been approached several times with offers of reenlistment, promises of bonuses, and promotion. I had decided I was through with all of it. I didn't want to leave my friends but I don't think could or would survive another tour.

I hadn't told anyone but I was just going to leave when I was done, disappear for a while. Where I was going to go I wasn't quite sure yet I would figure that out when the time came but I knew I needed to get far away from everything I knew.

I'm not sure how much time had passed while I had been sitting and thinking. It must have been more than I thought. Everyone was asleep in their bunks. It almost sounded like a symphony as everyone was snoring.

Listening to the silence and the snores was calming and then the mosque started playing prayer music. My silent reflection was over. The only thing that came across my mind when I heard the music was hate.

A hate for this place, hate for the helpless people who couldn't take care of themselves, hate for the brain dead idiots following the orders of radical fanatics, and just in general hate for everything over here. I let myself calm down as I lay in my rack.

I put my ear plugs in and tried to rest so many thoughts crossing my mind it was hard to set my mind at ease. Trying to quiet my mind was a battle but I finally won and fell into the dark.

12

TIME FLY'S EVEN WHEN YOU ARE NOT HAVING FUN AS LONG AS YOU ARE BUSY

The HMMWV's and Seven Tons started to drive off base with all of us. I looked at all the buildings as they went by and all I could think was how I hoped I would never see any of those buildings again.

Once off base every one gave a loud cheer as we were headed to our C-130 flight to start our trip home. I watched as we passed the farms and local villages. I started to think about Omar and his family.

All he wanted was a better life for his family, a life without fear, without starvation for his family, and with opportunity for his daughter. I wondered how many more families out there wanted that and how many were allowing the insurgents to hide among them because they were too scared to do anything.

The trip to the C-130 was shorter than I thought it was going to be. But I think that was because the drivers were going fairly fast. That and the fact that we didn't have anyone shoot at us or try to blow us up for once. This was a nice change of pace being the last trip.

Once we got to the C-130 we all got on and it took off to Kuwait where we would wait for our flight home. I always hated waiting in Kuwait going to Iraq and coming back home. I wish it was just one long trip instead of split up.

Once we landed in Kuwait we off loaded our gear into the tents. My squad pretty much just took off once released. They wanted to be the first in line to the fast food places on the base. I chuckled to myself as they practically ran.

I wasn't in such a rush I did want to have something deep fried or greasy maybe ice cream I wasn't sure but I would get to it when I got to it. It wasn't going anywhere and I was going to take my time getting there.

By the time I made it to where it looked like everyone was at, the outer food court, I could see pizzas, burgers, and tacos. I don't think anybody had grabbed any healthy food. I looked around and hoped I would see Chap or Joker but didn't see them anywhere.

I stopped at the ice-cream shop and ordered a double scoop of dark cherry in a bowl. I sat to eat the ice cream and noticed in the 120 degree weather that it was melting pretty fast. I ate it a little faster than I should have but still slow enough to enjoy it.

As I was finishing and looked up I saw Joker coming my way. I spoke as he sat beside me, "Hey buddy. Have you seen Chap?" Joker just shook his head no but didn't respond. I spoke again, "You alright? You seem down."

Joker answered, "I'm good I just still feel off. I'll be fine. I just need to get home and be away from everything for a bit." I responded, "I hear you. I can't wait to have leave and just be away from everything."

Both of us just sat in the food court not doing anything but watching people come and go as they got food ate and left. It almost felt surreal as I watched everyone come and go almost like I was watching them and also watching me watch them.

I could almost see myself sitting at the table with Joker then I could also see everyone moving around me but as if I was floating above watching like I was flying.

I guess I must have spaced out because next thing I knew I was being choked from behind by Chap as he caught me off guard. Squeezing fairly tightly and holding for a second Chap finally released me and I could breathe again.

As Chap sat next to me I punched him in the shoulder fairly hard. Chap just chuckled and started to eat the hamburger he purchased. Joker stated to talk about his family and the things he had planned when he saw them.

Chap and I just listened to Joker talk about possible planned trips and things he wanted to do. I almost envied what he had to go home to. Don't get me wrong my family was awesome but I didn't have kids so it was different.

Chap and I had nothing to go back to but our parents and siblings after my first tour being with my family already wasn't the same. They hadn't changed but I had and trying to fit in was difficult at best. Having conversation was forced and wasn't enjoyable sometimes. I feared questions and having to give answers. I just wanted to be left alone. I have learned to put space between myself and from everyone to protect them and me. It protected them from me lashing out at them or saying something I didn't mean and it also protected me from flash backs or an unnecessary mood change.

I didn't get further into my thoughts before Chap was pulling me up by my collar. I stood up as Chap pulled. Chap didn't say anything he just patted my back. I then followed Chap and Joker where ever they were headed to.

They lead me to the Tents I hadn't realized how late it had gotten. It was hard to tell time here with how long the sun stayed up. Even at 9:00pm it was still bright outside. We were leaving early in the morning so I decided to sleep to make time fly by faster.

I did a quick head count and my squad was all accounted for so I laid down in my rack to rest. It didn't take me long to fall asleep. This was unusual maybe it was a change in scenery or maybe I was just that tired.

It wasn't long before my sleep was interrupted by fire watch. It was time to pack up and fly out and once packed we headed to the briefing room and were debriefed. We all started joking about the warnings they were giving us as we walked out.

We were warned not to drink too much because it had been so long. We were warned to stay out of fights and confrontations. They warned us about dealing with civilians and to limit our exposure until we were cleared mentally.

We all knew it was all a joke. They didn't really care. They were required to give the warnings because they were liable for our actions if they didn't. They knew things would happen. That wouldn't change from the briefing.

The only thing that changed was they were no longer responsible because they had adequately warned us what not to do when we got home with a 45 minute brief. You honestly think we were going to listen to a brief on the way home and remember it. Takes a certain kind of stupid I figured to believe that.

It didn't take long after the briefing to have everything ready for the flight. Like I thought they went through all our bags again. Two of our guys didn't wipe there cameras apparently and got them confiscated. I laughed you could screen all you wanted stuff would get out eventually.

Once all our gear was scoured we packed it all back up and loaded it into the quad con for the flight home. We loaded up onto the commercial flight and for the first time in a while I felt air conditioning hit my face as I walked into the plane.

As usual I walked into the far back and saved a seat for Chap and Joker. But unfortunately they didn't sit beside me. Two other marines then filled the seats next to me. A little frustrated I just moved as close to the window as possible and decided to sleep the flight away.

As I was trying to sleep during the flight I could hear everyone starting to get rowdy. Someone had smuggled a bottle of alcohol on the plane as usual and was sharing it. I just brushed off the gestures of the marines next to me to join in and tried to go back to sleep and putting my ear plugs in for good measure.

The next time I awoke we were landing in South Carolina on the military base. I woke to everyone cheering and screaming that we were home. After the plane landed we were escorted to busses which drove us to camp Lejeune.

What I liked best about the drive into Camp Lejeune was how the family's showed their support by making huge banners and had decorations everywhere where the busses were coming through and stopping.

As we got closer to our drop off location we were informed to meet at the barracks the next morning and not to be late. All everyone was talking about was how hung over in the morning everyone probably was going to be at that formation.

As we stopped and everyone got out, I watched as fathers hugged their little daughters or sons or both. Wives were kissing them. What most everyone didn't know about me was I was going through a divorce. I kept my personal life mostly to myself. My parents didn't even know I was married for almost a month before they found out.

Coming home doesn't hurt your heart until you have had something to come home to then no longer do. On the other side of the fence were all the single marines. They were all talking about the party they were going to have and how much they would drink.

Everyone seemed so excited and happy except me. I knew what coming home was. It meant my purpose and drive was over. My ability to fit in and be normal would be gone all over again. I would be stuck back in the cycle of drinking.

I must have been giving too many emotions away on my face. Chap came over to me and placed his hand on my shoulder and spoke,

"It's going to be alright bro. I know what you're thinking and I feel it to. Let's go to the bar."

I didn't wait to check in with anyone. Chap and I just left. Chap got in his truck and tried to start it. But the battery was dead from sitting for so long. We both lightly chuckled and I pulled out my phone that I hadn't used since the deployment and called a cab.

We went to the bar that we had been frequenting for a long time. I wanted Joker to come but he was occupied with his family. Chap on the other hand already had an ex and knew how I felt and had no one to greet him so we just had each other.

A lot of the family's had been welcoming and even invited us to come with them as we were walking by. But it just didn't feel right. I just wanted to sulk in my grief and sadness. I wanted to take a good bottle of whiskey and drown out everything I had been through.

My mind was shot I was tired I didn't have

anything here I wanted to be around and see. I looked up and saw the bar coming into view. I looked over at Chap and I recognized the look on his face. I started to wonder if coming to the bar was a good idea as we got out of the cab.

Both Chap and I were obviously in a mood. I hoped the drinks would relax us and cool us off. As we sat on the back patio an unfamiliar face came to our table. As the gentleman came over to serve us I could see his name tag said Dean.

I spoke as he stood there patiently waiting, "Two double jack and cokes." The waiter just nodded his head and walked to the bar. I spoke to Chap as Dean walked away, "A waiter that doesn't speak maybe? And I wonder what happened to our old bartender? Where did she go?"

Chap just shrugged his shoulders as we watched the wave's crash onto the beach. I tried to soak in the sound as it crashed over and over, repetitiously beating the sand in a soothing sound. I could almost sit on the patio forever. It wasn't often I was relaxed like this.

The waiter came over to our table and handed Chap and I our drinks. I held up my credit card and as he took it I said, "Tab." The waiter just nodded and kept walking to the bar. Chap propped his feet up and slumped lower in the chair so he could stretch out.

I took slow sips of my drink to enjoy and remember its beautiful taste. As I swallowed a chill ran down my spine and I got pins and needles on my face. It was a good feeling and bad at the same time. I started to wonder if I was going to start my spiral into drinking again or if I could hold it off.

I gripped my drink tightly flexing my muscles in my hand and took another sip. Chap started chuckling to himself as he started to sit up and spoke, "Quit being self-absorbed and relax. You think too much and it shows on your face sometimes you just have to not think."

I cracked a smile and spoke, "You know me too well and you are right." Chap spoke, "of course I'm right I'm always right. Now quit ruining my woossahh time and relax. I just smiled and leaned back in my chair and took a deep breath.

The air was salty and cold but it was so nice out compared to where we had been. It was so nice to know I could sit here and enjoy myself with nothing to care about and no one to worry about. As I drank the last bit in my glass Chap ordered another round.

We stayed at the bar drinking for a few hours just relaxing to the noise of the ocean. I decided although I liked the sound and view of the bar I no longer liked the server so I called a cab. As I hung up the phone Chap spoke, "What's up?" I responded, "I don't like this place anymore. Let's find another place with the same view."

Chap didn't argue with me and we both got into the cab and left back to the barracks. Chap spoke as we got close to the base gates,

"Why don't we just buy our own stuff and just drink in the room. It will be cheaper that way."

I just smiled and nodded my head. Cheaper meant we could drink more. Chap and I managed to score the same room in the barracks. We hadn't even seen our room yet nor unloaded our stuff. All of it was still in his truck.

They had taken our guns and other gear in South Carolina when we were getting on the busses. So there wasn't much we had besides our cloths and boots now. It would all be re issued when we got back off leave.

As we both lay in our racks I decided I didn't like my rack and moved my pillow and blankets to the hard floor. After shifting around a bit I could hear Chap chuckling at me. I just ignored him and tried to go to sleep.

I could hear all the noises of the barracks. I forgot how annoying it was in the rooms. I tried to block the noise out and finally had to get my ear plugs to stop the noise. After my ear plugs were in it didn't take long for me to fall asleep.

13

THE FIGHT OF A REAL HERO NEVER TRULY ENDS FOR HE SACRIFICES TOO MUCH

Things seemed to be moving along smoothly for me getting out of the Corp's. Chap hadn't talked to me in a few days. I think maybe he thought I was abandoning him. Chap had planned to reenlist in the next month or so.

I had a psychological evaluation to pass before they would finally let me go. I had been transferred to Head Quarters battery for my EAS. It was a lot different than what I was used to. We still ran every morning but I had no job duties or training to do.

It was pretty much stay out of sight out of mind and chill in your room until you were officially gone. No one really wanted to have anything to do with someone getting out. This was fine by me. I had been honing my drinking skills during the day and video game skills at night.

I'm not sure what had happened to Joker. I knew he was having a rough time with his family but he wasn't talking to anyone about it. I think he was having a hard time adjusting to his family and vice versa. But it was hard to tell without him wanting to hang out anymore.

Chap said he had something planned for me but I wasn't quite sure what it was. I was assuming it was a big send off party of some sort. I had less than a week to leave assuming I passed the evaluation this afternoon.

I had already collected my DD-214 I had laughed so hard when I picked it up. There wasn't much information on it. Then I laughed even harder when I tried to get copies of my medical records. They had apparently disappeared while I was in Iraq during transfers.

It wasn't like I needed my medical records to get out anyway. I was starting to miss the Chow Hall in Iraq the food on base was pale in comparison. It just chased away the hunger and breakfast was the only meal worth eating.

Chap had already gone back to living off blocks of cheese and meat. I had been starving myself a few days out of the week. Not intentionally but I just didn't feel like eating. I could tell my mood was changing. I had also regressed back to avoiding everyone except Chap.

It wasn't long before my alarm clock snapped me out of my daze. I looked at the time and knew I had to get going to my evaluation. I had been coached how to pass it. I knew if I didn't pass I couldn't leave and I didn't want that to happen.

Once I got to the office I wrote my name on the pad at the desk and took a seat. There were a few other Marines in the waiting room with me. Out of all of us in the waiting room I was the only one in uniform.

Everyone else was dressed in civilian attire. You could tell a few of them had not shaven in a few days. The sight of these marines disgusted me. How could you let yourself go that much? I half thought about saying something to them.

Then I decided they weren't worth my time. They obviously didn't care either way. I'm pretty sure someone has said something to them along the way and they still looked this way. Not long into almost changing my mind. The lady behind the desk called me up next.

I was lead into a room with a desk and two chairs. It made me feel uneasy as there was also a window I couldn't see through joining another room. I started to wonder if there were people on the other side watching me through it.

I didn't have to wait long before a man in a white coat came in. He sat in front of me already looking at me and writing notes down. He started asking questions about my tour. I was pretty vague on my answers. I was told not to be direct and give a lot of possible or not to be direct for my answers.

The man in the white coat started asking me about my thoughts and feelings on my deployments. I just told him I went did my job and came home what feelings are there supposed to be? I wasn't sure what he was looking for.

All I knew was no matter what I cant answer I think about ways to exit a building in an emergency, or I have night mares, or I have weapons hidden where ever I sleep, or flash backs. I wasn't allowed to have any of that and get out. So of course I was going to lie my ass off.

After about and hour and half of the man in the white coats questions he finally let me go back into the waiting room to await his verdict. I don't think I had been that anxious and nervous in a while. One slip and he would fail me and I would have to reapply.

After waiting for almost an hour the lady at the desk called my name again. As I came to the counter the handed me a slip of paper saying I was sane. I chuckled to myself as I walked out like I needed a piece of paper to tell me.

If I evaluated myself I would have labeled me certifiably insane or at least eccentric at best. I had never been normal to begin with anyway. I folded up the paper and left to go find Chap. It was getting close to 4:30pm and he should be getting off about now.

Chap met me at my new room in the Head Quarters barracks. There were a few guys there with him. Some I knew some that didn't. I could see they had ropes and a roll of duct tape. I looked at Chap and spoke, "Do I need to ask?"

Chap smirked and spoke, "You haven't been branded yet and you leave real soon. The boys decided since you didn't do it yourself we were going to make you do it." I laughed and responded, "I'm not going down without a fight."

They all smiled as they got closer and Chap spoke again, "We wouldn't have it any other way." They all jumped me each trying to hold down an arm and leg. I got a few good swings in and made a few connections.

But in the end there were too many of them and I was over whelmed. A few of them proceeded to hit me back for the hits I got in as they duct taped my arms and legs so I couldn't move. Once they had me sufficiently taped up they put me in Chaps Truck.

Chap had conveniently taped my mouth as well. He never said where we were going but I had an idea. Chap started talking as he drove, "I'm disappointed that you didn't take the reenlistment package."

I would have responded but the tape was still on my mouth. As I looked out the window I could see people were starring. I started chuckling to myself as I starting getting a few ideas to screw with people.

Chap looked over as he heard me chuckling and looked at my face then spoke, "So you want to pretend to run away and freak people out do you?" I gave an evil like chuck as to respond yes. Chap spoke again, "alright make it look convincing as I will make it look real enough this might hurt.

We both started chuckling to ourselves as the traffic came to a stop at the red light before the main gate to get off the base. I was able to stretch far enough that I could open the door of the truck. Chap had already released my seat belt.

As the door popped open I tried to hop out and hop away as fast as I could. I didn't get too far. I couldn't imagine how funny it looked as the other marines on base just sat there watching me try to go to God knows where.

It didn't take Chap long to get me. He didn't even fake hit me and gave a good gut punch and whack to the head he then threw me over his shoulder and walked back to the truck to my amazement no one came to help.

As the traffic started moving and we got off base. An officer who had been watching us must have been speeding to catch up to us. He demanded we rolled down our window. As Chap did the Officer started yelling at us on how this wasn't funny.

Chap just laughed that much harder. The officer demanded our unit and names but Chap obviously gave false information. I would have been laughing in the officers face had my mouth not had duct tape on it.

It didn't take long for the officer to give up his banter of questions and there was nothing he could do to us as we were already off base. Hopefully he wouldn't recognize Chaps face later as for my face I didn't care I was getting out anyways.

Once we lost the officer Chap started driving to where he was going originally. Once we got to an empty field he pulled the duct tape off my face. I spoke, "Shit man it's about time." Chap responded, "It's good for you to be quiet for once sometimes you talk too much."

I just chuckled and waited for whatever Chap had planned. He was digging through his truck for something but I couldn't see what he was digging through nor the items he was pulling out. As I waited I got out and hobbled to the tail gate of the truck and sat on it.

Once Chap got what he was looking for he sat beside me with a small bag. Chap spoke, "Tonight's about you and everyone we have served with whether they were lost to us or not, tonight is also about the ones we will lose in the future."

Chap pulled out a bottle of Jack Daniels and several shot glasses. He poured the first one and spoke, "This is for the ones we lost." Chap poured the shot in my mouth and spoke again, "This is for the ones we are about to lose." I took the second shot. Chap spoke again, "This is for our memory that maybe none of us will be forgotten." I took the shot and Chap started speaking again, "Lastly this is for you and may you never forget."

After the fourth shot Chap helped me back into the truck and started driving again. When we got to where we were going I kind of laughed as a few of the guys were already there waiting on Chap and I to arrive.

It was a hole in the wall Tattoo Parlor. As I came to the doors of the tattoo parlor the guys came over to me in a circle. As the started taking the duct tape off me they took turns punching me in the gut and arms. I just flexed my muscles and took it.

Once they were done taking the duct tape off me and they were satisfied I had been beat enough we walked into the tattoo parlor. They must have already paid the guy because he was already at the chair waiting for me.

I knew what to do I had gotten a tattoo before. I just never got my Marine Corps tattoo. As I sat the guy shaved the spot for the tattoo and sanitized it. He then got to work and as he started it burned a little like my last tattoo did but then the pain was replaced by an adrenaline rush that got me going and mixed with the shots I had taken earlier it almost made my head spin. Two hours passed and it was over and my tattoo was done. I got into Chaps truck; I could feel my ribs and abs as I sat down in his passenger seat. Chap started driving to the bar where everyone was waiting for us. Once we got there the guys already had a table set out and chairs for us to sit in.

As I sat in my chair the bartender came by with drinks and shot the guys had ordered for when I made it there. We made a toast to great friends and took the first set of shots. I sat and soaked in the atmosphere around me.

There were all sorts of different music playing. My buddies were playing rounds of pool and a few were playing darts and about every 30 to 45 minutes one of them would buy me a shot to drink along with whatever I was already drinking.

I just sat and enjoyed the ride watching everyone have a great time. Chap spent a lot of his time beating everyone at pool as hard as I tried I couldn't get Chap off the table either he was always a better pool player than I was no matter how hard I practiced.

The bar tender called last call everyone minus Chap and I. We got into Chaps truck and drove back on base to the barracks. Chap pulled up to my barracks and let me out. He laughed at me crawling to my room as he got back in his truck to leave.

The Marine on duty for the barracks came out and helped me to my room. He looked at the fresh spot for my tattoo and laughed as he spoke, "Finally got branded. It's what you get for not getting it earlier marine."

I chucked to myself but couldn't find the energy to talk I was too drunk. He was right though. If I had gotten it on my own it would have been a lot nicer. I knew it was coming. Maybe I wanted it this way deep down. I wasn't sure. As the door to my room shut behind me I laid down on the floor the room spinning faster than I could keep up with. It was a tornado at first then silence, it all stopped and the darkness came quick and swift.

14

YOU CAN KNOW WHERE YOU ARE AND STILL BE LOST

Everyday seemed to be the same from the day before; wake up in the morning send in resumes to places trying to get a job and do some chores around my parent's house... wake up try to find a job and do some chores... wake up work on the job thing and do more chores. I wasn't sure what to do with myself now that there was no direction. I had always had something important to do, goals to reach, people to take care of. Now, I was unsure, what exactly do I want to accomplish? The only thing I really had on my plate was finalizing my divorce. I had an amazing lawyer who was doing it practically free for me because he loved to sit, listen, and talk about my stories.

So what did I want? What was I going to do? I didn't have the answers. I do know that I wanted a job. I had money so that wasn't an issue. I wasn't in a rush to actually get a job I just wanted one for something to do. The money I saved on deployment plus the extra I made doing dirty work there was more than enough.

I hadn't been home long but it had been long enough that it was getting a little uncomfortable. I wasn't sure if maybe they had heard me scream out in the night. They seemed to tip toe around me and not try to cause trouble or rile me up.

I did notice I was getting fairly aggressive. I had also been drinking more than I usually did which was already a lot. A friend told me to see the VA about my nightmares and I had made an appointment. Maybe they could give me the help I had been looking for since after my first deployment.

"Can someone help me in the kitchen?" I tried not to laugh as my mother interrupted my thoughts. She knew I was the only one in the house. She always tried to make it feel like an option to do it when there really was no option.

The smell wafting down the stairs was making my mouth water so I headed up the stairs and sauntered into the kitchen, I could see my Mom was already working on lunch. I had a pretty blessed life and one of those blessings was my Mothers cooking. My great love for good food maybe comes from a family who knows how to eat well. My mother always seemed to know what to cook just to cheer me up and from the smell of what she was making I would say it was homemade chicken soup, I peered into the pot, sure enough it was. I loved the smell of a house full of food. As I tried to sneak an early bowl full before it was quite done my mother smacked my hand with the wooden spoon she had been using and then shook it at me.

I just chuckled and started washing the

dishes she had used in preparing lunch for everyone that was coming over. I was nervous. It was my first holiday out of the Marine Corps. I hadn't had Christmas at home in a while.

The last few Christmases were in what I started calling the sand box. We even made a sandman with a plywood Christmas tree. I started to chuckle to myself as I thought about it. My mom spoke up, "What are you laughing about sweetie?"(Very southern accent) I chuckled again and spoke, "Oh nothing, just remembering decorations from the sand box last Christmas.

My Mom spoke again, "You just put that place out of your mind, we are going to have a wonderful time, and make new good memories. That can help you to forget about that horrible place." I just smiled and didn't say anything.

To be honest I was feeling a little hurt inside. You don't just forget and you can't. I didn't expect her to understand nor did I want her to so I just didn't say anything. She was only trying to help. But there are something's you have to work out yourself.

Some of my Mom's friends started coming in, neighbors, and other people I wasn't familiar with but had met before. I started to get agitated and annoyed. I had learned I wasn't comfortable in a group of more than four people.

I snuck out of the room back into the basement and disappeared for a while. I could hear everyone laughing and having a good time upstairs. For some reason this made me angry I wasn't sure why. All this family and I still felt alone.

As I sat in the basement my mind started to flash back to when I was in Iraq. In front of me were the faces of the people that I saw die, my hands dripping covered in blood, the blood running down my arms, I looked up as in prayer and tried to shake the devilish tugging feeling of despair and desperation for escape off. The walls were closing in on me, my vision becoming blurred, and the darkness was coming for me! That feeling surged and got so strong I was in a panic, tears began rolling down my face and I was crying and didn't realize it. I didn't know what this feeling was and I didn't like it at all. I felt helplessly lost and alone. It was that idea, that something stupid, where was this coming from?

I found myself playing with my Great Grandfather's 1911 .45 pistol. I didn't even realize I had pulled it out

And... I had already loaded it, the safety was off... I felt pain, regret, anger, lack of control. The darkness was surrounding me, separating me, covering me... it's so dark I couldn't see who I was anymore and my purpose? What is my purpose? I used to have a purpose but what I thought my purpose was I no longer had. I missed my friends they understood me, accepted me, I don't feel judged, and we had the same purpose. I'm feeling so very alone out here in a non understanding empty place of nothingness. Why didn't I stay in? Would it have made a difference if I did? What am I doing? I could hear laughter, I took a deep breath and I could smell good food, I thought about Jonathan as I looked at the pistol and felt the loss. I slowly unloaded the bullets and put the gun back in the case.

I made it through the moment and whatever that tugging feeling was it is gone now. I forced myself to get up and I decided to drown myself in alcohol and numb my mind. I had a stash all over the house. It was my way of coping at the moment. I had nothing else, my friends are all in the marines and No one here can begin to understand what I was going through. They would occasionally say things like I get it or I understand. Those words rung hollow to me and only made it worse. How could they understand? They hadn't seen or been through anything like I did. Words couldn't even explain the actions I did or why and what I had seen and experienced. It made me feel angry that they could possibly think they could understand the horror, the pain, the suffering, the agony, the fear we had to conquer, the darkness I felt was in my soul deep down where not even God could wash it away. There was no one I could trust to listen and not judge because they hadn't been through it. I needed someone who had been there to listen. No one here had that... they couldn't see. No matter how bad they wanted to... the connection couldn't and wouldn't happen.

My brothers had come down stairs to hang with me at this point. They couldn't even tell anything was off. I am a good cover artist and they will never know, because I won't let them know, the horrors I'm feeling. I bury them deep inside where they wait... in the dark.

We started playing Call of Duty together and my mind started to ease up. I enjoyed playing video games with them it was like putting yourself out of mind and into the game. Nothing existed except the video game and I grew to rely on these moments with them playing video games to drag me out of any hole I got myself into mentally. It was getting harder to pretend I was okay around everyone but the games helped the most.

Time seemed to slip by while we were playing video games and the next thing I knew it was time for dinner. My brothers and I headed upstairs and sat at the table. It was a fairly large crowd full of family and friends. I did my best to avoid conversation but every one still seemed interested to get information from me. I had gotten good at giving vague answers. If I couldn't give a vague answer then I was quick to change subjects. After a few prodding questions everyone seemed to get the hint I wasn't talking about it.

We were almost finished with dinner when Chap came through the front door. Chap was like a brother to me and my parents considered him a son. He didn't bother knocking because he knew he was a part of the family and whenever Chap came over he would just walk right in.

My Family greeted Chap with Hugs, handshakes, and a few pats on the back. Chap must have caught some familiar look in my eyes and waived for me to go outside with him. I left the table and headed out the front door onto the porch.

Chap handed me a cigarette and spoke, "Hey bud, what's going on. Don't lie to me either I know that look you had at the table. You might be able to fool everyone else but you are not fooling me."

I took a long drag from my cigarette before speaking, "I'm good now I just needed some air." Chap just gave the you are full of shit look but didn't say anything. He just lit his cigarette and blew his smoke in my face.

I waived the smoke away and spoke, "I'm glad you made it down for the holidays. When do you have to take off?" Chap smiled as he answered, "Does it matter? I'm here at the moment. I'll leave when I leave.

We both headed to the basement. My parents had a nice set up in the basement; there was a full bath to the right when you came in through the garage, to the left was an area set up with a poker table and foosball table, and as you continued in there was a dart board on the wall to the right, a little further in was the Pool Table which was by the back door, and then to the left of the pool table was the large screen TV and gaming center with a leather couch.

It did much to impress any guest and was also my favorite room in the house. Not just because of all the things to do but mostly because the atmosphere of the room was very relaxing at least that was how I felt.

Chap being his usual self spoke as he got to the pool table, "Rack'em bitch." As I racked the pool table Chap pulled out a bottle of Jack Daniels he had in his bag and poured both of us a strong and very large glass of jack and coke. We played pool for an hour or so before my brothers joined in to play with us. Chap as usual won most of the games. Then once we got tired of pool all of us started playing foosball and after about an hour of Foosball we were all sitting on the couch just drinking.

Chap and I were the only ones left awake since both my brothers were passed out on the couch in front of the TV. Chap spoke, "So how about you tell me what's really going on." I shrugged my shoulders as I started to speak, "I don't know what's wrong to be honest with you I'm losing my mind I guess because I can't sleep right, I still have night mares, and they're only getting worse as time goes by."

Chap smiled and patted my shoulder jokingly as he spoke trying to lighten me up, "That all?" I cracked a smile and spoke again, "I think the worse two things that have happened so far. Was my brother and I were filling up at a gas station, I went to pay the clerk at the counter and had a flashback of when we were clearing houses. I got lucky no one got hurt but my brother had to drag me out of the store.

The second time I was at a bar with my brothers and I'm not sure what exactly happened but from what my brothers said I ended up smashing some antiwar sissy with a chair. He apparently was provoking me and like I said I can't remember much. Needless to say I don't leave home anymore if I can help it."

I took a big swig from my glass then continued talking, "It's got my family worried and scared though. They don't say anything but I can see it in their faces from time to time." Chap spoke, "You should be lucky to have the family you do."

I nodded agreeing with Chap and refilled both our glasses. Chap spoke as we continued drinking, "I'm being moved to another unit. It's close to here so I'll be visiting when I can." I responded, "My family would like that. I'm moving up to where my dad is working but we will come down every weekend."

Chap spoke, "I see how it is. I find a way to come see you and you bugger off." I lightly laughed as I spoke, "It just worked out that way. I didn't know you were moving closer. You're family so come when you can and I'll see you when we are both here."

I shook my head in agreement and just continued drinking. Chap went over to the couch and rolled both my brothers off so he could sleep on it. I laughed lightly as I went upstairs to my brother's bed room and went to go to sleep on his bed.

I felt better after talking to Chap it wasn't that he changed anything it just made me feel more secure when he was around. I tried to go to sleep, to quiet my mind, but random bloody and sand covered body parts kept flashing across the window screen of my closed lids almost like spirits trying to haunt me. I reached for my drink I had brought up with me and chugged what was left of it down and tried to lie down again. The alcohol started to kick in and the room started spinning as I closed my eyes. I smiled as I got the result I was looking for and let myself fall into darkness.

15

NO ONE KNOWS BETTER
THAN YOU

Things seemed to be going really well for me at the moment. I began working in Construction with my Dad, currently we are working in Chattanooga Tennessee. I had gotten back on my feet and was working hard which felt good. Working with my Dad and brothers in construction seemed to bring us closer together although I had forgotten what slobs they were. We were living in a one bedroom apartment together and there were always cloths everywhere. On our days off I would clean and straighten most everything up with my Dad. My brothers however couldn't seem to be bothered.

I've had a few touch and go moments at work. I tend to be overly aggressive compared to what most people are used to. One guy at work wasn't paying attention and ran over a ladder with his bob cat that someone could have been coming down. I nearly ripped his head off and pretty much scared the shit out of him. I don't think he had been yelled at like that in his life. I did end up apologizing to him later for over reacting but civilians didn't understand that type of correction to bad behavior.

I had yelled at dozens of boot marines like that and they didn't bat an eye but yell at any civilian like that and most of them drop and cry. I started calling it soul breaking, I was a great leader to those I liked but I tended to soul break the ones I didn't want to be around.

I had met a girl online that I had been talking to. She seemed nice. She definitely talked a lot but I liked listening and I didn't have to say much. She had talked to me at work and seemed to think my angry outbursts were funny when I screamed at my guys in Spanish.

I didn't speak Spanish fluently by any

means but I knew all the words they would understand that meant I was pissed and they should be productive and get moving. If all else failed I would find my brother to be a translator he spoke Spanish better than I did.

My trips to the VA and calls to the VA went without success. I was sent away and told that I didn't qualify for assistance. I wasn't sure what to do other than do it on my own. I obviously wasn't getting help with the system that was supposed to help me.

With no ability to get my medical records and the VA refusing to help me I started to feel betrayed. I fought hard doing the job I was told to do. I didn't want to be there the politicians wanted us there and now that I'm back from serving my country and need assistance to get fully on my feet I'm considered trash and thrown aside, no one wanted to help or assist me. The only reason I even had a job was because of my family I wouldn't even have that if I didn't have the family I had and I would be homeless or worse.

I tried to clear my mind. I was starting to get frustrated again. I decided to call that girl I had been talking to she seemed to be able to calm me down. I noticed I was less prone to doing something I regretted after talking to her. She had a special way about her that made me put things going on around me into perspective. What was nice was when I told her the truth about myself and how I was she didn't judge me or run away. Even in my worse drunken phone calls to her she seemed to just want to talk me down out of my anger. There is always so much anger.

After talking with what I started thinking of as my long distance girlfriend. I noticed I missed a call. When I called back it was Chap he told me that Frank had been killed in action and that he wanted me to hear it from him first.

My heart sank. I didn't have much else to say other than ask how he was but the words were hollow and didn't mean anything. Chap knew there was nothing else to say and hung up after saying goodbye.

It didn't feel that long ago that Jonathan had taken his life. About a few weeks ago I had also learned that Daniels had killed himself with a shotgun in the mouth. All the friends I lost in Iraq now with Frank adding to that long list.

A sudden depression washed over my body. I could feel it from my head to my toes. Pins and needles were everywhere and I felt nothing but sadness. I punched the wall next to me a few times and then myself in the face. I flew into a rage.

I texted my dad to tell him my work was done and I was leaving the job site. He said that was fine in a message back. It didn't matter I was already on my motorcycle and gone. The only place I could think of where I wanted to be was the bar.

I had been texting my girl in-between red lights. She had promised to talk to me but was tied up with her work. I didn't tell her what exactly had happened but she had dealt with me before like this and started to catch on to when I needed to be talked down.

The last text she sent me was to not do anything drastic until she could get away and talk to me on the phone. She forced me to promise and I did. But that didn't mean that I couldn't get drunk and sulk in my own pity party by myself.

I sat in the corner of the bar back against the wall as far from anyone as I physically could get. I started ordering double vodka and red bull. I usually only did that when I was looking for a fight. But I wanted the red bull to give me an energy boost.

I was so dragged down at the moment I just wanted to cry myself to sleep but the Marine in me told that pussy personality to fuck off. I went numb my emotions now gone. I had done that before and more often now that I was out.

So I tried to man up and ordered a few straight shots of Jack Daniels one for each of the friends I had lost and started taking a shot and toast to a memory of each of them. I didn't take the shots back to back but did take one almost every ten minutes until they were gone.

I found that if I separated my emotions and thoughts I could get by regardless of how I felt. But then I generally turned into what everyone seemed to be calling an ass hole. I was just being logical with no filter on my mouth a lot of people don't like the straight truth though.

I had been drinking by myself for a few hours now. I had lots of time to think and cool off my thoughts. My phone rang and it was my girlfriend. I answered the phone. She sounded relieved that I even picked the phone up.

As we talked I explained how my day went in detail to fill in the gaps and how I was now at the bar. I told her about my friend and how I was having a hard time with it. She comforted me the best she could over the phone.

I didn't realize how long we had been talking. But I decided I should probably pay my tab when I saw how many glasses had piled up on my table. I think the waitress was too scared to take anything off of the table.

Once I paid my tab which was well over one hundred dollars. I headed to my motorcycle. I grabbed a few things out of my bag and took my helmet. I started walking to my apartment. The whole time I was amazed how this girl wouldn't let me off the phone.

Here I am being a total douche bag drunk not caring about anyone but myself. Yet she still wanted me to hang onto whatever honor I had left. She was a really good distraction or at least it think she is maybe I am just that drunk.

At that time I realized I had been walking in the wrong direction towards my apartment.

When I told my girlfriend she started laughing at me. I'm not sure but maybe it was her laugh that lightened me up. I couldn't tell too many emotions still going on.

As I turned around I noticed a police officer had been watching me walk beside the road. As I told my Girlfriend this she started to flip out saying I was going to get arrested. I told her to hold on as I put the phone on speaker and in my shirt pocket.

It didn't take long for the Police Officer to pull up next to me as I was walking and he spoke, "Where are you going?" I responded, "Home." The Police Officer spoke again, "Where's home?" I answered, "Another half mile ahead of me the apartments on the corner."

The Police Officer now spoke more stern, "How much have you had to drink son?" I replied in a smart-alecky tone, "Enough to get this Marine on his way but not too much as I could have then drove home instead."

The Police Officer spoke into the radio for a moment then spoke to me, "I respect that you didn't drive and you better not decide to drive like that in the future. I'll let you off with a warning this time. Next time get a taxi or a designated driver."

The Police Officer drove off. I smiled to myself as I picked the phone back up. My Girlfriend was still freaking out but was glad I didn't get arrested. I just kept laughing and was now in a better mood as I continued on my home.

It didn't take much longer to reach the apartments. My brothers and my dad were already asleep. I continued to talk to the girl on the phone and I could feel the alcohol really getting to me as I lay down. I tried to talk more but fell asleep as I tried listening to what I now considered the angel on the other phone.

16

TO HEAL ONE HAS TO START AT THE BEGINNING

I can't believe how fast time flies. I have been working so much and filling the rest of my time in-between at the gym. Adjusting to civilian life is damn near impossible. What I have learned to do is work in a bubble and only let select people around me.

I'm in the process of selling everything. I'm leaving everything behind I can't get rid of. I decided that I need a fresh start somewhere new away from so many reminders of my past. I was able to trim myself down to a jacket one pair of shoes and a set of cloths.

I'm' excited and scared at the same time. I'm excited for the change and to get away from everything. I'm scared about the what if's. What if the change doesn't help me?

What if it doesn't work out with my fiancée?

She says she loves me and knows everything about me. I confessed everything to her. I wanted to be honest and up front. But how long could she stand being with me? Would it turn out like my last marriage? Would she give up on me?

These were all questions racing through my mind. I had asked my girlfriend if she would marry me and she had said yes. Everyone told me I was rushing it but I felt in my heart I wasn't. To be honest I wouldn't be alive if she hadn't come into my life.

I had already hit rock bottom and all the times I had thought about committing suicide she had convinced me otherwise. She knew I had a lot of issues but I never told her how close I had gotten to just ending it.

Then like an angel she made everything start going back to normal. I still wasn't sure what it was she was doing. All we did was talk but all I looked forward to was hearing her voice and seeing her today for the first time on Valentines Day when she flew in.

I must have been talking to her for several hours a day and I had never texted that much in my life. I was starting to feel like I was borderline obsessed but I started to think this obsession is what was carrying me on.

I had woken up early this morning and had hand crafted a card for her. I could have bought one but I thought a really well done one by hand was more personal and I had gotten her a stuffed tiger with a leather Jacket to go with it.

I think my family was getting a little irritated with my obsession with my fiancée, I didn't care this was about me and her and no one else. I think they were maybe upset with the fact I was moving so far away. It's hard to tell what bothered them most.

I know they just wanted what's best for me and I knew this move was. The day was moving by so slow... Time had been flying by until today. I was watching the clock until I was to meet her at the airport and it was taking forever.

On the plus side it gave me lots of time to plan and get everything set up for when she arrived. I had everything in the basement set up already. We had tons of different types of drinks. My mind was still racing I couldn't seem to slow it down.

I hadn't had my adrenalin rushing like this since I had flipped Chap off the back of my motorcycle when we were showboating around. I hoped she would think I was what she expected we had never met in person before.

It was quite the leap in faith going on just phone calls and text messages but if we built a bond strong on just that then the bond in person should be even better I wasn't sure what to expect. I had seen pictures but it is quite different in a picture than it is in person.

For the first time since I had been out of

the Marine Corps I had been happy all day nothing could seem to ruin it. I haven't been depressed at all and normally it would come and go throughout the day.

As I sat and thought about this I prayed this change would last forever and I was bound and determined to do everything in my power to hold onto this change. I knew in my heart it wouldn't be like this forever but I would ride it as long as it lasted.

I did things around the house to pass the time and I came up with more ideas for things to do. It got close to time to leave. I wasn't about to be late to the airport. I don't think my family grasped how important this moment was to me.

They kept saying don't rush and you have time. I'm never late to anything and early to everything. This would be no exception. I wanted to get to the airport early and plan in my mind how I would greet her and where.

I wanted everything to go perfectly and I

was going to make absolutely sure that it all went how I wanted it to. I decided to put the gifts in the back seat and left to the airport. When I got to the airport it was a lot more crowded than I thought it would be.

I could feel my anxiety rising and I started to grit my teeth to bear through it until I found a spot that I was comfortable enough in to wait. As I looked at the flights from the time line I still had almost two hours before she landed. I walked around finding the possible ways she would come out.

Once I found the stairwell she would most likely come up I then positioned myself far enough away I could gauge her reaction to look for me and also give me enough time to recognize her first. Would we hug right away or go straight for a kiss? I had a few ideas going through my mind and I wasn't exactly sure how I was going to do anything then decided to just roll with whatever happened. As I patiently waited it was as if time had frozen, the plane was about to land and I was getting more nervous by the moment.

I started having second thoughts; What if we didn't get along in person like we did on the phone? What if I had a flash back in front of her would it scare her away? I started to feel that anxiety again and had to force myself to calm down. I had to act normal I was not going to let my broken mind to ruin this for me. This was my chance to start a new life and make it. I had to make this work I refuse to be a statistic. This would work, this had to work, and I was going to make this work.

I already loved her just from our conversations I was going to do whatever was necessary to insure this was successful and failure was not an option. Per chance if this did fail I planned on disappearing from everything I knew maybe not permanently but for a long time at least.

I was getting riled up again I needed to cam myself down this was supposed to be a happy moment. I was supposed to be excited not getting angry. I took a few deep breaths and stated to calm down. She should be showing up any second I wanted to be smiling. Just as I got calm I could see her face as she came up the escalator then her body. My first thought was, damn she is short but as short as she was I thought she looked beautiful. The pictures she had did not do her justice.

She didn't see me at first it took a moment as I started towards her for her to see me but when her eyes met mine she knew who I was and ran straight into my arms. It was the first time since boot camp when I received my eagle globe and anchor that I felt that much joy as she held onto me.

We began to move on to the car and as we walked she went right into talking. I was too entranced with watching her walk to hear all the words she was saying as she looked at me, I just nodded and smiled. I helped her carry what little she had brought thinking how great this was and how wonderful this was going to be.

I had thought about kissing her several

different times but couldn't find the right moment or approach yet. I could tell she was getting a little nervous and was expecting it. We had talked about it over the phone and I had said it would be the first thing I did. However I got cold feet when she hugged me, I missed my opportunity then.

The whole drive to the house she never missed a beat as she talked about work, family, and her home. I could tell she was trying to make me relaxed and was leading the conversation deliberately as we continued on our way I tactfully gave her the gifts.

She seemed glad and impressed at the way I not only presented it but what I had done with the card. It made me feel good that she appreciated the effort I took to make it. She said the Tiger suited my personality well.

As we got to the house and walked in. she greeted my family and we had dinner already set out for us. After we ate the majority of the time was spent drinking and having a great time in the basement with everyone.

As the night came to a close I could tell she enjoyed herself. There was one thing missing I still hadn't given her a kiss as I had promised. I told her to hold out her hands and close her eyes. As she did I moved into kiss her.

She opened her eyes just as I went in and we ended up bumping heads. She laughed ad asked if I was trying to kiss her. As I said yes she grabbed me by my shirt and pulled me in for a kiss. I could feel my face tingle and my hands felt on fire after the kiss she had asked what took so long. I explained that it had been so long since the last time with my ex-wife and she was the last kiss I had. I wanted to make sure it was right and I didn't want to screw it up even though I screwed it up anyway.

We spent the rest of the night cuddling and talking on the couch. I was flying back with her when she was leaving this would be a new journey in my life and I hopefully would be leaving my nightmares behind me.

I started to fall asleep with her in my arms

I felt a comfort that had eluded me since childhood. I felt comfort and as the world around me got darker all I had left were a few thoughts as I fell asleep. I wasn't sure how it was going to go but I was going to give this woman everything I had to make a happy life for both of us. I still had issues but I think if I take my battles one day at a time with the future love of my life helping, I hopefully would have a future worth living.

GLOSSARY

C130- Heavy transport plane

MOS- Trade label for what you did in the military

USO- Military version of a convenience store

M249 SAW – Light machine gun that carries 200 round magazines

IED- Improvised explosive device, anything that was used to make a bomb

EOD- A team that goes out and disables IED's

Dip- Tobacco you put in your lip and let it soak. You absorb the nicotine through the skin.

MRE- Meal Ready to Eat, Super concentrated food that lasts a really long time and if consumed to much can ruin your digestion.

HMMV – is a hummer H1 model military style. Armored on doors and windows is weak underneath and on the roof.

7Ton- Is a rally big troop transport vehicle. No armor for troops carried in the back however.

Mortar- An infantry used shell for medium distant targets kill radius range of approximately ten feet depending on the round used.

Bunk- Where you slept and kept you belongings

Bunk house- where two or more of you kept your Bunks, Could be a shack or better.

Mosque- Religious prayer building Muslims pray in.

Chow hall – Where we eat

On post – this is used to describe when you are guarding a position usually in a tower.

On duty – used to described when you are guarding a barracks or equipment

Devil pup – term used for some one who is new or fresh to a situation or the marine corps.

Gear- what you kept with you to keep you ready for any situation.

M16A2- Semi automatic rifle, every marine has one.

1911 .45- An older model hand gun that packs more than the average punch

M240- Heavy machine gun

AK47- light machine gun

Kevlar plate- Armor used to protect your front and back from harm

Salt dog- A marine who has been through something rough at some point in his carrier if not multiple times.

HQ- the place in which orders came down from some times this was not your own command some times it was.

Insurgent- Terrorist fighting to cause fear

in any way they can. There goal to in flick as many casualties as possible even at the cost of their own death.

POST STORY

Chap has been to the nut house for attempted suicide but is doing well for himself and has a family.

Joker committed suicide while his family was trying to get him help and is no longer with us.

I Married that girl in the story and now have a daughter. I still deal with my demons on a daily basis. The fight never truly ends. But what I've learned is to make sure I have something worth fighting for. My wife and daughter are what drives me forward. Without them I would have lost my battle long ago.

Several more of my friends which stayed in and had a more tours in Iraq and Afghanistan never made it back. I have lost 3 friends to Iraq and 2 to Afghanistan after I got out.

As I am writing and completing this book

the Veteran suicide rate is 22 Veterans a day. I have had 3 friends commit suicide. All of the friends I talk to have either thought about it of attempted suicide at some point after combat service.

Even more are homeless and either can't keep a job or can't get hired due to discrimination or their Post Traumatic Stress and TBI.

The help available has denied and abandoned too many veterans that are in need in Canada and the United States.

I am one of those vets that have been denied. If not for my family I would have been a casualty to.

CREDITS

I'd like to thank my parents for being supportive in the worst and best times. I couldn't have had better role models on family values. To my wife Mandy, who has been my everlasting support and best friend. I owe you every day of my life. You truly are my heart and soul for without you I would have neither. To my mother and father in-law, not sure how you put up with me, but I am grateful for all you do. To all of my Marine friends who helped me keep the stories straight. Especially Thomas Bailey brought back good and bad memories. Special thanks to Bob Bagosy and my Uncle Jeff. Thanks for being my judges on my writing. You input meant a lot.

"© 2014, George Adam Day. Except as provided by the Copyright Act October 2, 2014 no part of this publication may be reproduced, stored in a retrieval system or transmitted in any form or by any means without the prior written permission of the publisher."

www.ingramcontent.com/pod-product-compliance
Lightning Source LLC
Chambersburg PA
CBHW051510120626
46551CB00012B/859